If you are a

small business entrepreneur

this is your story............

SALLY,

Always protect your
DREAM!.

It's Your Frog …
Warts And All

Published in 1999 by
Biznet Publishing Company Inc.
3427 Forrestdale Circle
Mississauga Ontario Canada

Canadian Cataloguing in Publication Data

West, Douglas Warren, 1946 -
It's Your Frog ... Warts And All

ISBN   09683931-0-1

1. Small Business   2. Entrepreneurship

Editor: Kim Arnott
Illustrations: Leroy Danclar
Cover Design / Page Layout: Brian Naidu.

Printed and Bound in Canada

FOREWORD

"For entrepreneurs every failure should be taken as an opportunity to learn."

There is nothing personal about failure. Failure is about options that didn't turn out, or strategies that didn't produce the expected results. This book is dedicated to the special people who wear the label of entrepreneur with pride, dignity and enthusiasm. Visionaries, dreamers, hard-working, practical, extraordinary ordinary people who make up their minds to put their knowledge, skill, drive and determination to the test by starting their own business.

The title of the book, 'It's Your Frog - Warts and All', refers to the love all entrepreneurs have for their business good, bad, or ugly. This is a story familiar to millions of small business entrepreneurs. Anyone dreaming of opening their own business will benefit from the practical lessons learned by one young entrepreneur as she struggles to build her business after she is downsized out of the company she thought offered her long term security.

The characters in the book are fictional but the experiences are real. The situations Cheryl finds herself in and the advice given to her by her friend, advisor and mentor Doug are drawn from real life experiences. Through an exchange of letters between Cheryl and Doug spanning a five-year period you are given a rare insight into the thoughts, emotions and experiences of everyday life as a small business entrepreneur.

In simple, matter-of-fact language, you are taken on a fascinating journey, as Cheryl encounters the challenges faced by entrepreneurs everywhere when trying to build successful businesses.

It was not my intention to write a 'how to' book on operating a small business. You will pick up proven and practical tips to help you improve your business, but the real intention of the book is to immerse you in the 'feeling' of being an entrepreneur. You will come face to face with a lot of the highs and lows, laughter and tears, angst and anxiety that is part of the roller coaster every entrepreneur buys a ticket to ride.

I hope you will find equal measures of information and inspiration in this book.

ABOUT THE AUTHOR

 **Doug West** is a small business entrepreneur, keynote speaker, and writer. He has over 15 years of hands on, practical entrepreneurial experience. He has lived through and experienced his share of failures on his way to success. He says of himself "I'm a young 50 year old, who has paid a lot of dues, but always enjoyed making the payments". Doug has acted as an advisor and mentor to many budding entrepreneurs, some who have gone on to build the business of their dreams, some who have gone on to try again. It is those experiences that were the inspiration for this book. Doug develops training programs, and conducts workshops on entrepreneurial management, leadership values and positive communicating, for a diverse client base throughout North America.

This book is dedicated to my wife Cheryl.
An extraordinary woman, wife and mother whose faith and quiet resolve never wavered along the long and winding entrepreneurial road. My inspiration for all the gentle and gutsy determination shown by the 'Cheryl' in this book.

Special Thanks To:
CHERYL CAPPELLANO my business associate for sharing her real life experiences, insights and anecdotes about small business. Her always positive outlook and inexhaustible good humor during the writing of this book, made the row a lot easier to hoe. Cheryl is the creative marketing force behind the promotion of this book, our workshops and other collaborative efforts.

Thanks To:
MY SON JAMIE who is the kind of guy I always wanted to be. **MY DAUGHTER MEIGHAN** who makes me believe in good and whose sense of fairness fills me with wonder and envy. **LIZ McCALLUM** for the consistent care and feeding of my fragile ego. **TREVOR GOSBEE** for 25 years of unconditional friendship. **ALEX BARROTTI** my compatriot in many early entrepreneurial struggles and forays.

THE LETTERS

It's Your Frog...

Warts And All

START - UP ANXIETY

Dear Doug,

Am I nuts? Maybe I should have just gone out and found myself another 'real' job. What makes me think I can start my own business? I'm a corporate animal, all my work experience has been with one large company. Sure, I'm not going in blind, I have experience in the market sector I'll be doing business in. I took a small business start-up course over the last two years, but that was for something I thought would be down the road. Never did I expect the road was going to get real short, real fast.

So, here I am flying to the other side of the country and about to become a small business entrepreneur. I'm supposed to be excited, so why do I feel so excitement-challenged? I feel like my emotions are sinking lower as the plane climbs higher. My positive resolve is rushing out of a crack in my emotional dam and the reservoir is being re-filled with anxiety. This sneak attack on my confidence began as soon as we said our good-byes and I became the occupant of seat B, row 17, flight 168 on the first leg of my journey from Hartford to Seattle. My fellow believers in heavier than air flight and I, are buckled up, some watching, some listening to, most ignoring a flight attendant as she goes through the in case of emergency, need to knows. I tune out about halfway through her dissertation on disaster survival and let my mind sort through all the different thoughts and images vying for my attention.

The dominant thoughts and images at the moment are of people places and things that used to be. It's like watching my own in flight movie, starring me. The movie is like a documentary with highlight footage of who I used to be and what I used to do. Or is that really one in the same?

The scene I'm seeing at the moment is me, back in the offices of Deezeyen Inc., the largest business interior design company in North America. Its the day three years after I started with the company, when I experienced my first tangible sign of corporate success, my own office. For some that may not seem a major cause for celebration, but having spent the first three years as an open concept cubicle dweller this first faltering step up the corporate ladder was very big indeed. There I stand at the door to the 8 x 10 piece of real estate that was to be the center of my at work universe for the next five years. I remember the satisfaction of reaching out to open the door - a door and walls and privacy, how could it get any better than this. Well maybe a window would have been nice, but that would come I was sure, with the next promotion.

The next scene that comes into focus is a typical day in my life as a senior accounts administrator. There I am, checking my voice mail, and my email. I'm playing voice mail tag by responding to the voice mail messages left for me by leaving voice mail messages for them, and answering email by return email. It's shaping up to be another typical '90s kind of corporate work day. There are always a couple of daily meetings I'm scheduled to attend. Most of the committees I'm a part of seem to meet to discuss whatever it was we discussed at the last meeting before we decide to adjourn and think again about what it was we discussed. God, I used to get so frustrated. How many times did I go home at the end of another spin the wheels day and ask myself why I put up with it. But on balance the good days far outnumbered the bad and in spite of it all, they were eight of the happiest years of my life. Great co-workers, some of whom became good friends. Like a lot of families, we at work shared the fun of things like birthdays and weddings, the joy of births, the concern over illnesses and even the sadness of deaths. It was on the whole a nice, non-threatening, if somewhat less than challenging workplace. But then there were lots of Monday mornings and Friday afternoons when I didn't necessarily need a lot of challenge.

Back to reality, here I am at 35,000 feet, but I sure don't feel on top of the world. I'm trying to remind myself that this seat is occupied by a successful, bright, energetic, articulate, good looking, and I might add modest 30 year old. A woman about to embark on an entrepreneurial career that will be the stuff of legend. Maybe written about in magazines and books, maybe even a movie? Cheryl's life story: maybe Jodi Foster playing me!

My emotions are bouncing up and down like the insides of a bungie jumper. One minute I'm having fun with my thoughts and they're splashed with vibrant neon colors. The next minute the fun fades and my thoughts turn to pale shades of gray. If I let my guard down feelings of sadness, anxiety and emptiness create a kaleidoscope of negative unsettling images. I can't remember if I've ever felt such an overwhelming sense of loss, sadness, and grief, combined with mental, physical and emotional exhaustion.

I'm trying to regain my focus and push the negative thoughts aside by, as you suggested, looking ahead at all the good things in store for me. But it's hard to see very far ahead with these damned tears in my eyes. I'm trying to concentrate on thoughts of good times to come, but feelings of loss keep getting in the way. I'm leaving behind friends, my job, my home, just about everything I guess I always thought was going to make up my little corner of the world. So many things have been left unsaid. Why do we have so much difficulty acknowledging endings? We say "so long," we make plans to visit, we promise to call, to write and to stay in touch. We are never ready to say good-bye, until the time for good-byes is too late.

The sights and sounds of the going away parties and the emotional freeze frames of the happy caring faces of friends and colleagues already seem to be losing their uniqueness and the memories are crowding together. I'm realizing a lot of good-byes to a lot of good friends are probably permanent, despite heart felt and emotional promises to stay in touch. And I know there aren't likely to be many, if any, yearly reunions. I wonder about what the future will hold for so many of the people who made up the fabric of my daily tapestry. My everyday people.

I'm already thinking of them as singular faces in fading still-life photos of my past.

A morbid thought intrudes, who's untimely demise might be the catalyst to reunite the group I already think of as my 'old friends'? Will there ever be new ones to take their place? Sometimes I think that after a certain age, say around 25, you never make any more really good friends. You make friends and acquaintances, but real good friends? I'm not so sure. Can you believe I'm writing this letter one hour into what you described as "my flight to freedom"? I wouldn't, at this moment, be a very good model for a positive thinking poster.

It was so much like you, and so nice of you, to come out to the airport to see me off. Thanks. I really enjoyed the laughter and the glass of wine we shared before my flight. I didn't look back to wave after we said our good-byes because I wanted to leave, as you said, looking ahead to my future and where I was going. Not back at where I'd been.

I've got to give myself a shake. I just re-read the first part of this letter. I think if I get any more melodramatic I can start writing for the soaps. Enough already!! I'm going to order a glass of wine, and strike up a conversation with my seat mate.

In three hours the first leg of my journey is over and in a few weeks, I intend to have Success by Design Inc., up and running and on its way to becoming the next great small business success story.

I'm back. I had a great conversation with the man next to me and I feel like my positives are beginning to percolate. We are about 20 minutes from landing and I only have a 30 minute layover before the final leg of the flight to Seattle, so I'll finish this up on the layover. I'll get this letter off to you as soon as I get settled at my friend Meighan's place. It's sure going to be nice having her around to help me adjust to my new surroundings. I don't know if I would have been quite so brave or prepared to make this move if she hadn't been living in Seattle and promoting it like she worked for the Chamber of Commerce. According to her, Seattle is the hub of the universe, big enough to be big but not pretentious and small enough to still be warm and friendly. She even insists it doesn't rain—all that much. She was able to find me a place to rent about 10 minutes from where she lives and I take possession at the end of the month. I can't wait to actually see what I'm going to be calling home for the next year. Knowing Meighan the place will be fine. I'm really looking forward to staying with her for the next few weeks and having her show me around. The next time you hear from me, I'll be calling you from my home office or as I like to refer to it, world headquarters of Success by Design Inc.

Cheryl

You can change your life in three easy steps:
1. start immediately
2. stick with it
3. refer to steps one and two

ENTREPRENEURIAL
DETERMINATION

Dear Cheryl,

I was waiting to hear from you before putting fingers to the keys and responding to the letter you wrote during your flight. That letter, said more between the lines than what was written on the paper. One of your comments during our phone conversation last week, really hit home. You said you hadn't realized just how emotional this whole experience was going to be. Then you said, you were worried that maybe you were too emotional and weren't going to be "tough enough" to run your own business. Let me tell you, tough is over-rated.

Don't mistake having feelings, and reacting to and being in touch with your emotions for weakness. I would describe the successful people I know as strong - not tough. They aren't afraid of their feelings, they're in touch with them. The cornerstone of emotional maturity isn't about being tough enough to deny, ignore or hide from your feelings, it's about being strong enough to work with them, appreciate them and enjoy them. Work with your emotions, not against them. People who are wound so tight that they will go to any lengths to keep their feelings in check are 'flat liners' destined to live their lives without life. Besides, what makes you think you're going to become Ms. calm, cool and collected with all that Italian blood running through your veins.

From what you told me the move appears to have gone well. It didn't take you long to get organized and settled in. With all this talk about the people and things you are going to miss, has it occurred to you yet how very much you are going to miss our splendid New England winters? You know, the ones you dealt with in your own unique style by attempting to remain cloistered indoors from December to April. I know you're going to miss the chance to keep us spellbound with your annual winter whine about the bone chilling dampness you claimed was aging your mind and body prematurely. Remember how you used to keep me laughing with stories about your attempts to 'manage' the winter by hibernating indoors between warm weather vacations. Good thing the pubs were heated or you might never have ventured out. Well from what I know of your new home, you definitely won't be dampness deprived.

One of the things I will really miss is the happy-hour gatherings with you and your colleagues and the interesting, fast-paced, funny and politically incorrect conversations that made them so enjoyable. The endearing habit you had of picking up my tab now and then, made them all the more enjoyable. On the up side, the fact that in your new business you will be working closely with restaurants and hotel dining rooms should bode well for my culinary adventures when I visit. I'll have my tailor let out the waist on some of my pants in anticipation of things to come.

I know change can be overwhelming and you have certainly had your fair share this past year. You experienced the downsizing of the company you had been with since entering the workforce; the only company you had worked for, and the place that had been the focal point for so much of your business and social life. The place where, as you said, you made your first grown-up friends and experienced a lot of personal growth. It's unfortunate that very often only in giving up of something do we fully realize what a wonderful thing it was we had. Doubly so, when the giving up is force fed to you. I hope though, through the process of writing your first few letters to me - including time outs to wipe away the tears - that you will be able to bring closure to a memorable and happy eight year chapter of your young life, turn a new page and move forward, to new challenges and adventures. I have to agree, now that you've moved across the country, you may find it difficult to maintain old friendships. But new friends are waiting to be made. You have your friend Meighan and some of your family there and a bright, 30-year-old woman, with your personality and myriad of interests, won't be sitting writing sad, introspective letters for long. New is to young as settled is to old, the time for adjusting to new is at your age, not mine. Just think of what it would be like for an aging boomer like me to have to adjust in similar circumstances. I'm not going to be trite and say that change is always for the better, but in your case there's no doubt it will be.

I recall our lively and animated conversation last year, when you first brought up the idea of opening your own business. Remember how impressed I was with the fact that you had been taking some 'how to start a small business' courses to get yourself prepared for, if you wanted to do it and when you wanted to do it. Well, the 'when' came a little sooner than you anticipated, but on the bright side it answered the question of 'if' for you.

I've always looked at change as being a combination of reaching out and letting go. For you, it's about the trade-off between the fun and excitement of creating a new life, in a new place, and the sadness of leaving the old, friendly, and familiar. You need to keep moving forward and looking to the future. That's where you're going to spend the rest of your life. You're too young to be remembering the good old days. Your focus needs to be on creating exciting new days.

Your eyes were sparkling when you began describing your business idea to me. Your excitement, was contagious. The words were dancing off your lips. That's when I knew you may not have worked out all of the timing in your mind, but in your heart you were already there. You were going to go for it.

A quick aside here. Don't ever let yourself forget that one of the reasons you've decided to open your own business is to enjoy a new and more satisfying quality of life. Don't let it become only a new but not very satisfying way to work. Too often, in my experience, budding entrepreneurs can get so quickly caught up in the quantity of work required to make their business successful, they forget their business is supposed to be the foundation to support a new and better quality of life.

Allow me a story to illustrate my point. You are much too young to remember this, but in the days when I was but a lad, there existed a group of service providers called milkmen. These hard working men would venture forth in the wee hours of the morning in horse drawn milk wagons. They would deliver bottles of milk, right to the doors of the houses of their customers. That's right they came right to your house! In those days you could if you wanted to, get your milk in an interesting bottle that had the cream sitting at the top supported by the milk. Nobody it seems was overly worried about fat content in those days. That bottle with the cream on top makes me think of how the life of an entrepreneur should be and too often isn't. All the hard work and long hours you put into your business should be like the milk in that bottle - there to support the cream at the top, the lifestyle and quality of life you're working so hard to attain and enjoy.

I'm excited about continuing my role, as you described it, of friend, mentor, and advisor. You flatter me (and I love it) by insisting that my thoughts and ideas will help you make your business the success you want it to be. Remember though, some thoughts may make more sense than others, depending upon the intake of wine over dinner, or the strength of my medicinal late night scotch.

My advice to you will not have much to do with what I call the 'hardware' part of the business, such as the how-s and why-s of your business plan, or finding the right accountant or buying the right office equipment. For one thing, you already know more about office technology than this techno-peasant ever will. When we went through your business plan, I told you I was impressed by how well researched and thought out it was. The financial projections are realistic and your marketing plan is fine.

What I propose to advise you on are mostly software matters. No, not which computer programs to buy, but the issues that speak to the heart and soul of operating a small business. The angst and the anxiety, the highs and the lows, the laughter and the tears: the everyday stuff of life as an entrepreneur. I want you to think of me not just as a brain to pick but also as the shoulder you may need from time to time. If we do this right, we are bound to trip over some practical thoughts or ideas to help you deal with the everyday issues that will confront, amaze and sometimes confuse you.

Two rules I insist on. The first; you will have to get used to and put up with some thought interruptions, idea wanderings, and general babbling, as my wife calls it. After all, I am now, as she is fond of reminding me, over 50, with the attention span of a house fly! The second; I want us to be able to talk and write to each other candidly and honestly with no punches pulled. I want us to set out on this journey together, as equals. I expect to learn as much from you as you from me.

O.K. then hitch up the wagons, let the journey begin. I think the best way to begin is to use some broad brush strokes to paint a picture of what the special breed of people we call entrepreneurs are all about. I believe that entrepreneurs are in many ways the modern day equivalent and spiritual descendants of the early pioneering settlers who made this country great. Think about it, can't you just picture yourself hitching up your team of horses to the wagon and starting out on another days bumping across the plains?

I'm not real sure about this pioneering stuff!

Those were very special people, they were prepared to buck the odds, knowing they would have to overcome tremendous challenges and adversity in order to build a new life. So it is for many of modern day entrepreneurs. Just as in those times, when people's determination, hard work, and faith in their abilities, often meant the difference between success and failure, so it is for entrepreneurs today. The early settlers moved across the land with drive and determination in search of opportunities and new outlets for their talent and skills. Is that really any different from entrepreneurs today, moving geographically and occupationally in search of opportunities to put their talent and skills to the test.

When you look at photographs of early pioneers you notice certain common characteristics in the way they appear. They have an unmistakable look, the result of long days of hard physical labor. When you look into the faces of people who have become small business entrepreneurs you notice that they to have an unmistakable look. New small business entrepreneurs are easy to spot; they are the ones with the look that can only be created by too little sleep, too much coffee, too many fast food dining experiences, a lot of anxiety, a dash of gnawing self doubt, a pinch of frustration and a whack of the scaries and worries. But in spite of it all, like the early pioneers they remain positive and optimistic about their new life and new opportunities.

Being an entrepreneur is about believing in yourself, even when friends and family begin to doubt you. There is a famous quote that I'm sure you are familiar with; "Some men see things as they are and ask why? I dream of things as they could be and ask why not?" I think this quote should be the rallying cry of all entrepreneurs. I have been privileged to know many successful small business owners over the years and one of the things common to each of them, was that they had all started with a dream of what could be.

Being an entrepreneur takes equal measures of thinking, feeling and doing. Entrepreneurs don't just love their businesses, they are in love with them. In fact, the emotional bond between an entrepreneur and his or her business is rivaled only by the bond which exists between loved ones or very close friends.

Entrepreneurs are unique, passionate, complicated, headstrong, self centered, egotistical, fun-loving, work-addicted, strange, puzzling and special people. They come equipped with a simple and I'm afraid, not very trendy, value system. They anchor their lives in a value system based on the belief that no matter the circumstances, and no matter the challenge, they will build something lasting and worthwhile for themselves and their families through their own initiative, drive and determination.

Entrepreneurs are part of the solution. They help fuel the engine that drives the new economic train. Small business entrepreneurs are the heartbeat and life blood of the new economy. They pick up the people wounded in the restructuring wars being waged by big government and big business. They help broken people become whole again by creating jobs for them. When small business entrepreneurs build businesses and create jobs, what they are really doing is helping to restore peoples faith in themselves, and in the system. giving them hope, and creating meaningful futures for them.

Small business entrepreneurs embody what this country is supposed to be, and used to be about. And yet they are continuously discriminated against by government and banks. It's always the big guys who get bailed out by government and banks when they screw up, never the small business entrepreneur.

Small business entrepreneurs rarely get a chance to burst out of the starting blocks in their race for success. Instead, they stumble forward, bound and blinded by the red tape that seems to be manufactured in endless supply by governments at every level. In fact, I believe that if red tape was a food source, the government with its inexhaustible supply of old-fashioned fertilizer, could grow a crop that could feed the world.

Being an entrepreneur is about trusting and testing your instincts, marching to the beat of your own drum and not dancing to someone else's tune. It's about using common sense to break the rules that make no sense. It's about making a commitment to quality in your life and in your business. It's doing what's right for you and your customers, because it's the right thing to do. And not because you have to, but because you want to.

Being an entrepreneur is about loving what you do so much that you would do it without being paid, which in fact, most do for the first year or two. It's about being so tired at the end of another week of 14-hour days that you feel two days older than dirt. Then, in the next breath, wishing you had more time and energy because you just want to go back and do it some more.

Entrepreneurship is about getting up in the morning and wanting to go to work, not having to. It's about having the discipline to go to work when nobody is there to know. And because the business is yours, it's about giving one hundred percent every day, even when you know most days you could get by on seventy-five.

Entrepreneurship is the new business spirituality being embraced by millions of people around the world. It's not just about being your own boss, it's about being your own person. It's about putting the living back in your life. It's about the challenge of creating a balance between work and play.

Through it all, it's about looking in the mirror and liking what you see. And in the end, it's about hoping it will never end, because as any entrepreneur will tell you, it's the most exciting ride they've ever been on.

Incidentally in case you think you are part of some small band of business misfits think again. Small business entrepreneurs are part of the fastest-growing sector of the world economy.

Small business entrepreneurs are part of the rebirth of individual innovation and accomplishment which was the hallmark of skilled craftsmen before modern workplace technology replaced individual pride and initiative with collective jobs. As of yet, no one has been able to locate a factory that produces entrepreneurs. There is no production line entrepreneurs come off of fully equipped with all the options they need to be successful. Entrepreneurs are individually hand crafted.

That's my overview of entrepreneurs. Now let's focus in and be a little more specific about what I think it will take for you to become the success you want to be and maybe put a little scare into the competition along the way.

Operating your own business is going to mean having to add some ingredients to your skills mix. You're going to have to blend together your administrative and management expertise with new skills in sales, marketing and operations. Successful entrepreneurs often begin their business because they possess a singular expertise. They are very good at some one thing they do. They soon realize however, that to build and operate their business they need to expand their expertise and become business generalists. An example of your becoming a business generalist is the need for you to develop the skills you will need in order to generate sales. Until now you have never been called on to uncover sales leads and make direct sales calls on customers. Now your new business demands it. What current strengths do you have that could be applied in the area of sales? Well, you are well organized, you communicate in a positive non-threatening way, you have a professional well groomed appearance, you are knowledgeable about your service, and you understand the common needs of your target customers.

Those are all important ingredients in your sales skills mix, but what needs to be added? You are going to need to learn how to identify and categorize potential customers, so that you don't end up wasting precious selling time. You will need to become comfortable making introductory sales calls. You will need to learn how to uncover customer needs and respond to them. You will need to learn how to conduct sales presentations to both individuals and groups. You are going to have to learn how and when to use the right questioning techniques in order to get information or commitments from your customers.

So you see, there is more to the success of most small businesses than building a better mouse trap and waiting for the world to beat a path to your door. You better be able to go out and sell it.

How can you speed the development of your sales skills. You can begin by reading books and articles on sales techniques and making note of how other successful people apply them. You can enroll in some sales skills training seminars. But most importantly you can learn by doing and from your mistakes. Nothing beats just doing it. Get going, go out and try to sell something to somebody. I've seen a lot of small businesses get off to an unnecessarily slow start because the person starting the business was reluctant to get out and sell the product or service. It is better to make the effort and fail than to fail because you didn't make the effort. Selling is an action game and a contact sport, as soon as the game begins you've got to focus on taking the actions needed to put you in contact with your potential customers.

Your comfort level in your new role of salesperson will increase in direct proportion to your competence. The more competent you become the more confident you will be, and the more comfortable you will become. Any new challenge you take on can be scary until you learn what to do and how to do it. So while practice may not make perfect, it will help rid you of sales call reluctance and help you keep the 'scarys' in check. One of the real keys to any successful transition from one skill set to another is to remind yourself that fifty percent of your success is going to result from attitude and fifty percent from aptitude. Nobody said it would be easy. Believe in yourself and go out and get it done.

Doug

The world is full of willing people. Some are willing to work, others are willing to let them!

GIVE ME A LITTLE CREDIT

Dear Doug,

I was a little surprised at the time it took me to set up my operating line of credit with a lender. The first two I went to acted like small business is a plague and I got the impression they would like to stay away from it. Three others gave me the impression that for them small business is some kind of odd economic phenomena that, with any luck, will go away. They weren't really excited about my business plan.

As you know I did my homework and put together a well-documented plan including my current financial statements, start-up costs, operating expenses and revenue projections for the first year and going out to five years, all put together with the help of my accountant. I included a profile of my target market and marketing plan and used everything I learned about developing a business plan in the small business start-up course I took at the local college last year. I had copies printed and properly bound so that they would project a professional image. As you know from the copy I sent to you I used the following format, dividing the business plan into three parts.

I began with an overview of my business concept which included:

- Positioning the concept and stating my business objectives, including a mission statement.

- Identifying emerging trends that supported a growing market for the service I was offering.
- Isolating the challenges faced by small business and those specific to my business.
- Media articles and statistics pertaining to the projected growth of the target market.
- Identifying the strengths and weaknesses of my main competitors.
- I developed a comprehensive marketing plan which included:
- Identifying the target market relevant to my geographical marketing and service area.
- Breaking the target market into the top 100 and secondary 100 prospects.
- Compiling a list of the top ten customer benefits of doing business with me.
- The five key components of my marketing strategy.
- Analyzing the expected needs of my target market customers.
- The initial customer contact methods I would use.
- A marketing and advertising launch strategy.
- The third segment of my business plan was of course the financial projections.

So it really annoyed me when, after all the work I put in, some of the banks brushed the plan aside and wanted to base their decision to do business with me only on the amount of personal start-up capital I was prepared to commit, and personal collateral. In almost every instance they wanted a list of what other personal assets I might have that I could pledge as collateral for my 'business loan'. In two cases after my personal finances were chopped and diced and put through their blender, they played their trump card, asking me to transfer all of my accounts, bank credit cards and my investment portfolio into one of their 'service packages'. I have quickly come to realize that there are no real business loans available to small entrepreneurs. What the banks offer are glorified personal loans.

I watch the commercials produced by these banks, and boy, do they ever hire very good people to put them together. Its obvious they spare no expense to produce some great heart-warming commercials.

According to the message in the commercials, they spend most of their waking moments caring and worrying about better way to serve their small business customers. Gee, I wonder if it's mostly a public relations gesture? Do you think? I guess they must be meeting and working on their big business strategies when the commercials are aired, and miss their own message.

In any event, a friend of mine suggested I try getting my financing from a venture capital broker instead of a bank. I didn't think they would be interested because of the amount of loan required. The ones I talked to didn't even want to look at anything less than $500,000. So they do make investments in small business, just not in mine. So, after six weeks of non-stop searching, disappointment and aggravation, I ended up with a small well secured personal line of credit from a local bank. I have never felt as financially exposed or vulnerable in my life. I know now what people mean when they say they have their life tied up in their business. I haven't slept much in the last week but this time its not excitement over the business its more a case of stress and anxiety keeping me awake.

On the upside, the phone lines are in and my computer, fax and email are ready to go. The business cards, stationery and brochures are printed. My very own business cards, which mean I'm in business, right? My home office is set up and the President's butt fits nicely in the chair. The company car is gassed up and ready to go. This entrepreneur is ready, willing and able.

Cheryl

BUSINESS CORNERSTONES

Dear Cheryl,

I can't say I'm surprised at your anger and frustration over trying to get a bank interested in looking at your business plan. What you have just experienced is creativity bumping heads with bureaucracy. I sometimes think if you just added three or four more zeroes onto the amount of your loan request you would have more chance of getting it. Don't blame the people at the branch level. As I'm sure they told you in most sincere, "I'm really on your side voice," it's just policy. Ah, policy, the impenetrable shield of super bureaucrats everywhere. I look at the business plan you prepared and wonder about the difficulties facing someone who may not have access to the resources that helped you put yours together. I've got to say, though, when you get on a rant, it is a beauty. Of course, you're right about all the heart-warming rhetoric the banks put out about their sincere, caring interest in small business.

Your comments about the commercials, at least the ones I've seen, are right on. They are very touching, very well done, and I would imagine, very expensive to produce. The production values are second to none. You've got to ask yourself, why would they spend that much money to promote their interest in small business, if they really aren't interested? To me, its right up there with the mystery of how they get the Caramilk into the Cadbury bar.

In spite of your run in with the vault vultures, you really sound pumped. I have a feeling, the business pace in Seattle is about to pick up. Your business cards and your stationery are terrific and your brochure is very clever and appealing. You should have good results with it as a door opener. Thanks for sending me the samples. I like the logo and I'm not surprised that you used yellows, blues and greens as your combination of colors on the brochure. Yellow to denote robust good health, blue to denote business efficiency and green for a calming effect Admit it you didn't think I was listening the time when you were telling me about the effect colors have on emotions. By the way, don't let the President's bum get too comfortable in that chair. In your business, you're going to find a direct connection between the time you spend out of the office and the business that flows into the office. I hope you have a good cell phone plan.

As for the banks, chalk it up to a positive, if frustrating, learning experience. You did persevere and you did find a lending institution that would work with you. Actually, your comments got me thinking enough about the situation to ask my banker friends (yes, I do still have some) why it is that big lending and small business seemed to butt heads so often. The commonality of their responses was that, too often, small business entrepreneurs come to the banks without having done their homework. As one put it, "You can't expect us to lend money on the basis of a business plan drawn up on the back of a serviette." I know that doesn't apply in your case, but I can see that they do have a point. I did remind the particular woman who made the comment about the serviette, that perhaps the banks could spend more money educating potential small business entrepreneurs on how to develop financially sound business plans and less on 'feel good' commercials. That just seemed to underwhelm her so we went back to talking about how difficult it is for the poor hard pressed banks to remain competitive in the global economy. You'll be happy to know I managed to hold back the tears as she related the difficulties they faced. It does seem, minor inconveniences aside, that you have things pretty well organized for the start up phase of your business. Your business plan is realistic, your funding is in place, your expertise is applicable to the business you are starting and your positive button is locked in the on position. Better call the success patrol and have them stand by to pick you up.

I'm going to focus the rest of this letter, on getting you to think about a couple of the cornerstones many of the entrepreneurs I know, have used to build a solid foundation for both business and personal success. You worked in a company that prided itself on its core competencies. The lessons you learned there are valuable, so don't forget them. I'm going to ask you to consider the benefit of weaving personal values and core competencies together in the tapestry of your business as it grows over the years. Try thinking of core competencies as the background cloth and personal values as the material you weave through it to create your personalized business design.

Core competencies are what you do best, the tangibles you bring to your business. In your case, that includes things like your creative design talent, and your administrative and operational abilities. Personal values are the intangibles you bring, like caring, pride, honesty, integrity, and a sense of humor.

Personal values are like a beacon, silently signaling to people, making them aware of what you're about and what you stand for. A simple thing, like having people know you stand by your word, is a powerful personal value. It's more likely to generate long term business than a ten page ambiguous guarantee ever would.

Personal values help your customers feel comfortable doing business with you, and they help you become comfortable with the way you do business. Your personal values will act as your moral compass and give you direction when things get rough. They'll compel you to do what's right, even when no one's watching. They will help you think in terms of what's right, not just what's right for you. Personal values, when properly chosen, create a sense of purpose for whatever task is at hand. They take the why out of why you're doing it, freeing you to just do it. They help you accomplish more in less time, with less stress. Personal values will help you set the standards for your everyday performance. They help you prioritize tasks and sift through information overload.

Strong personal values simplify life's rules and regulations and make them more manageable and understandable. They bring order to the chaotic Mad Hatter's tea party we attend most days. They help you swim against the prevailing current and take a stand for what you believe in. They build moral permanence into your life. Personal values encourage you to have the strong faith in your abilities you need, when you expect and demand winning performances from yourself. They will give you the drive and determination to compete and achieve at higher levels. They will also give you the self confidence to expect success, not be surprised by it. Pretty strong stuff from a few little intangibles, wouldn't you say?

I thought I would close this letter with what I call a personal values starters set. If you don't need it, pass it along to someone who might.

- Always try to respond to people in caring and thoughtful ways.
- Listen with passion and genuine interest when asked for advice.
- Have some compassion for the other guy and try to understand before passing judgment.
- Always try to do what's right, just because it's the right thing to do.
- Make a genuine effort to relate to people as they are, not as you wish they were.
- Feed on the positives around you and be a carrier.

That's it for now, but remember values come in two parts. First, are your declared values and second, the values you live by. For a lot of people, the declaring their values is easy, its the ones they live by that seems to tussle their tunics. Try not to have too big a gap between what you say you are and what you show you are. I think Emerson said it best this way, "what you are shouts so loudly in my ears, I can't hear what you are saying."

Doug

ADJUSTING TO
NEW SURROUNDINGS

Dear Doug,

Things haven't improved much since I talked to you on the phone last week. I feel totally lost. This time not in the emotional sense, this time it's directional. I just can't get my car pointed in the right direction half the time! It's times like this I realize my first big mistake in life was not completing my girl guide program. Yes, I know, the sun comes up in the East and sets in the West, but out here most of the time when you look up the only sun you see is in liquid form. The sun here seems to be a distant relative to the sky, showing up only on special occasions.

I'm running all over town, with my map book at the ready, spread out for handy reference on my lap or propped up in the passenger seat. On the upside I do get a lot of time to study the maps. I've never seen traffic like this, it seems like I'm in constant gridlock. I'm seeing way more of the geography than I need to and I'm starting to feel a little stupid because of the number of times I have had to phone from the car and have someone guide me in to where I'm going.

I'm late for appointments and you know how unsettling that is for a time freak like me. Probably not real impressive to the people I am calling on either. Everyone seems to understand though and they're understanding when I tell them I'm a recent arrival. The pace of life and business here is very vibrant with an attitude of 'lets do it' in the air.

It seems a bit more open and adventurous than back east. This is so much more of a doer than watcher lifestyle. Must be all the caffeine coursing through everyone's veins from the specialty coffees everyone here consumes. One quick observation, a lot of the people I've met have moved here from other areas of the country, just as I did, most, it seems, during the last ten years. Meighan must not be the only one singing the praises of Seattle. You know how organized I like to be, so finding myself lost on the way to appointments or having to make adjustments to my schedule is driving me a little nuts and that drive is getting shorter everyday.

As I said on the phone to you, last week, you, my friend, are way too scary sometimes. You seem to have a sixth sense that enables you to know what I'm thinking and feeling. I sat down over the weekend and re-read your letters about entrepreneurship and personal values. It was just what I needed. Just think, for the price of a postage stamp or the time it takes to email you a message, I can get instant therapy. I love it. I'm enclosing some photos of the Presidential office, and of the new me. I decided with all the changes going on in my life I might as well go for it and change my 'look' as well. Bet you didn't know I even had a 'look' did you?

Cheryl

WORKING   FROM   HOME

Dear Cheryl,

Not to worry too much about your situation driving you nuts, as you put it. You'll get through it with at least a few grains of sanity left on your beach, just like the rest of us did. I'm satisfied to know you could stay awake long enough to get through the last couple of rambles I sent you. I'll make this a short one, and try to do a little more teaching and a little less preaching. Keep those kind words and letters coming - an ego like mine needs a lot of care and feeding. The photos you sent of the new you, look terrific. That's quite a dramatic new hair color and style you're sporting. It gives you a very sophisticated, very 90's look. But what do I know? I've been combing my hair the same way for fifty years, and the only color change has been from black to gray.

The photos of the interior of your home office also look great. The office set-up seems to have turned out pretty well and I see you've managed to make it as bright as possible. The color scheme looks easy on the eyes and that's a little thing a lot of home office entrepreneurs overlook. The way you have it set up looks very functional and it should suit your needs for the immediate future. You can go the designer office route when you move up and out. And don't panic, as far as I know, there is no apparent shortage of rosewood furniture or Persian carpets looming on the horizon. It appears you have set up your office so that you can be productive and that's what's important. Look on the bright side, you won't be in there more than 16 hours a day anyway.

I reviewed your business plan and it calls for you to be out of the house and into a commercial site around the end of your second year. Trust me, those 24 months will go by like you're roller-blading downhill. You did write your business plan to be a guide for you to follow, didn't you?

Creative Problem Solving!

I remember when I started out working on my own by converting my extra bedroom into my home office. A lot of people thought I had two big advantages. One, I wouldn't have to sit in traffic listening to the traffic reporter on the radio tell me about the traffic I was sitting in any longer. (By the way, isn't 'traffic reporter' an oxymoron? Shouldn't it be 'gridlock reporter'?) The second big advantage everyone thought I would have was that I would be able to work in my jammies all day. The only guy I know who had any success doing that was Hugh Hefner, and I'm not sure whether it was working in his jammies or the inspiration around him that made the difference.

People were right on one count, but wrong on the other. I always maintained a business schedule, which included being dressed in casual attire. I was usually in my office by eight. Now granted, the 20-foot down-the-hall commute could be made, with coffee cup in hand, in about 10 seconds, even accounting for wife, daughter and dog traffic. But what was important was the way I felt: I wasn't running a home office, I was running an office from home.

My advice to you when you work from your home office is pretty simple. Work from your office and don't conduct business anywhere else in your home. Dress for the office, in casual comfortable attire that's one of the advantages of home based enterprise. Maintain regular working hours, which may sometimes mean 10 or 12 hours, but it also means breaks and lunches taken away from your office. Take a sixty minute fitness or attitude adjustment break everyday. You're an entrepreneur break some of the rules. Set up a working schedule that meets the demands of your target market and is flexible enough to taker advantage of working from home. Clear up what needs to be put away at the end of the day and when not in your office, keep the door closed. For most home office entrepreneurs, the most difficult problem is not going into the office when they should, it is STAYING OUT of the office when they should.

That's it for now. One more thing, almost everyone who works from home finds that family and friends call or drop in whenever they have some free time. They do it because to them you don't have a' real job', and you don't work in a 'real office'. Watch out for these well intentioned time bandits. Explain to them that the operable word in working from home, is working.

Doug

GETTING OUT OF ISOLATION

Dear Cheryl,

I neglected to mention on the phone the other day that I think the townhouse you've rented looks great. It's just what you need while you get settled and into your new lifestyle. It has that great area on the second floor where you've set up your office and you still have some living space. Your little private patio area will be a great place to take your breaks and sip your morning coffee and evening glass of wine, if it isn't raining, that is.

What's this mention in your letter about having joined a fitness and tennis club? Don't you know, according to page seven, paragraph three, subsection five of the small business entrepreneurs rule book, it is expressly forbidden to take any time off or have any fun for at least the first twelve months of being in business? Watch out, you are blowing the carefully-crafted and jealously-guarded image of the 16-hour-a-day, 7-day-a-week home office entrepreneur.

You may start a dangerous trend and people might actually start to consider some play time to balance the work they are putting in. What an odd concept, but all kidding aside, you've done a very sensible thing. You know what I tell people in my seminars all the time: "Work hard at work and work extra hard at creating some time to play." It's amazing how many people have become brainwashed into the 'work forever and always' syndrome. All work and no play definitely makes Jack and Jill dull, and inordinately boring. Remember all the animals with the exception of man, know the principal business of life is to enjoy it.

This is probably a good time to consider broadening your scope a little and looking for some good business networking groups to become involved with. As you know, my own group, the Small Business Success Network, has been very valuable in helping our members increase their referral business and promote their business by way of relationship marketing. I thought I would expound on the importance of relationship marketing in this letter.

Relationship marketing is an increasingly important business skill for small business people to learn and become comfortable with and proficient at. If you are in business today, you need to seek out and plug into opportunities to get face to face with customers from predetermined market segments.

Seminars, association meetings, service clubs and networking groups are a few of the venues that offer everyone organized and consistent opportunities to meet face to face with potential customers and referral sources. I know this won't come as any surprise to you Cheryl, because you have mentioned it in previous letters, but the complexity of the way businesses are interconnected today means we all need to be connected with a variety of groups in order to build our prospecting, customer and referral bases.

Interacting with people in a wide variety of groups enables us to stay current on a number of topics and issues, as well as position ourselves to take advantage of unplanned business opportunities that arise from the people we meet. This is doubly important for people like us, Cheryl, because we work from relatively isolated environments like home and small business offices. I think anytime we can take advantage of the opportunity to meet regularly with fellow business people, everyone involved is likely to benefit.

One of the keys to successful relationship marketing is to take time to learn some details about what the other person's business is, what it offers, what their philosophy is in running it and how they generate most of their business.

Find out what their interests are outside of their business, and most importantly, what you can do to help them. The getting-to-know you, breaking-the-ice and developing-a-rapport stage of business relationship building enables you to match the person's product or service to people you know who might need it. The benefit for everyone is that if you bring the right people together, you save everyone time and effort. You also gain respect and credibility in the eyes of both parties. Give the seeds you plant time to grow. Any exchange of information between you and your new business colleagues may not lead to immediate payoffs, but if you plan to be around for a while, it will.

Sound and profitable business relationships take time to nurture. You won't have much luck trying to build a base of lasting contacts if you have dollar signs flashing in your eyes and are always on the hunt for instant economic gratification. Don't measure the success of your networking or relationship marketing efforts solely in terms of how many immediate leads or sales you walk away with. To create long-term, vibrant businesses, you and others in your group have to take relationship marketing beyond the 'if you give to me, I will give to you' stage. Searching only for instant mutual reward undermines the 'we', and the 'us', in any group and places it squarely on the 'me'. This will lead eventually to people getting together not to participate in an environment of relationship marketing, but simply to trade cold call leads. Networking or relationship marketing meetings are not just about the number of business cards collected at the event or how many people you told your story to. Instead judge the result of the time invested on the basis of what you learned, what ideas were shared and what mutual challenges were discussed. Don't assign yourself some arbitrary number of new contacts to make at each meeting. Use the time equally to make new contacts and continue with the relationships you established previously.

Also remember to lighten up some. People who misunderstand the real function of relationship marketing and networking are often sent into uncontrollable frenzies at the thought of missing out on one potential sales lead who may have been at the meeting. Entrepreneurial zeal is great, but do yourself and other right thinking business people a favor by tempering your enthusiasm. You don't have to approach every human interaction as a potential life-and-death struggle for business.

Ah, the joys of familiarity, be it in what we eat, what we drink, what we do, where we go, or who we know. Familiar is comfortable and comforting. What it isn't, in business, is very productive. Don't narrow your business focus and spend all of your time with the same old people, in the same old places, talking about the same old, same old. Association groups are great, but if you are a banker or accountant or software programmer, don't just hang out with members of your same species. When you only interact with your professional colleagues, your view of the world can become pretty narrow. Broaden your base of networks and associates: it could give you a different outlook on an issue or a problem. Participating in a number of diverse business and social groups will expand your connections and create opportunities you may have overlooked or not considered at all.

I'm including a list of networking tips given to me by a colleague who has built most of his business through contacts he made in various networking groups.

Where: Ask entrepreneurs in your area about groups they would recommend. Most groups will invite you out for a look before you join.

Why: Network to build business contacts and to meet and develop friendships with like-minded business people.

How: You network most effectively by listening as much as talking. You can increase your networking results by developing an interesting, one-minute explanation of what you do and how you do it.

Hints To Make Networking Work Better For You:
- Be prepared when you attend meetings.
- Be open minded to what others do and think.
- Don't be afraid to ask.
- Treat everyone in the network as an equal.
- Don't waste your time or the time of others.
- Give without demanding a return.
- Set realistic goals of what you expect.

Doug

MY NEW BEST FRIENDS

Dear Doug,

I took your advice and looked around for a good networking group to hook up with. You are so right about missing the daily interaction of working with others and about how empty and isolated you can sometimes feel when you are working on your own from home.

There are certainly some different philosophies out there when it comes to business networking. I looked at the Chamber of Commerce in this area, but I think I'll wait until I'm a little more established before I consider joining it. I looked at some service clubs, but I think I will do my volunteering as I always did, by getting involved in a cross-section of participatory events. There is one organization with small chapters that are limited to one member per business sector. That seems like a good idea, and the people at the meeting I attended seemed very professional, knowledgeable and dedicated to making their businesses successful, but I don't think the group has the right mix of businesses for me.

I found the group I was looking for when I attended a breakfast meeting as the guest of one of my townhouse neighbors. He runs a small desktop publishing business from his place. The group meets about every six weeks and has breakfast in a meeting room in a restaurant about 15 minutes from where I live. There are about sixty members and they are a real cross section of start up and established small businesses. The meetings begin at 7 a.m. and we mix and mingle over a buffet breakfast. Then one of the members or an outside guest speaks on a small business issue for about 20 minutes. After the speaker each of us has a one minute opportunity to stand and remind the others of who we are, what we do and what type of customers we are looking for. The meetings usually wrap up about 9 a.m. I like the mix of small, medium and large businesses represented and the price is reasonable, so I'm now an official member of the "One plus One makes Three" networking group.

Cheryl

If you think no one knows you're alive,
try missing a couple of car payments.

EIGHT KEYS TO SUCCESS

Dear Cheryl,

I'm getting such a great kick out of this long distance mentor role. Best non-paying job I've ever had, and believe me when I tell you, like every other entrepreneur, I've had a few. All kidding aside, I think it's a privilege to be asked to share in the formation and growth of your entrepreneurial experience. Of course, you do realize my reputation is at stake. After your business has grown, as we both know it will, I will have to humbly come forward to take at least 90 percent of the credit.

I'm busy putting the final touches on another book and continuing to conduct my seminars, so there may be a short time lag between letters, and email, but I will answer as quickly as I can. I thought this would be a good time to review some of Doug's 'Guide for the Successful Small Business entrepreneur'. I know, I know, you're trying to control your excitement. In any event lets go once more through my basic mantra for small business success.

I am in business to generate a profit. Great concept right? Nobody I know in small business thinks there's anything wrong with profit, but it sure seems easier to forecast than attain. One of the reasons for this is that small business entrepreneurs, especially in the beginning, really tend to undervalue themselves and, in some cases, give too much away under the guise of business promotion. How can anyone put a value on your services, if you don't? Too often I've heard small business people tell me they can't afford to walk away from anything. Yes, there are times when this philosophy might apply, but don't let it become a permanent way of doing business. Generating revenue without profit is the fastest way I know to find yourself back in the 'I work for someone else' sector.

While local conditions may vary, I realize basic business rules apply to everyone, everywhere. I have to find customers. I have to sell my product or service. I have to provide value for the price I ask. I have to continue to grow my business on manageable terms. I have to generate profit. In order to build a loyal customer base, and reap the rewards of referral business, I must provide products and services with value equal to or surpassing that of the cost to the customer. For too many years, businesses of all types put their focus on generating a constant flow of new customers, while often taking for granted the customers they already had. The old 'once we get em', 'we'll probably keep em' mindset applied. Now it seems everyone is waking up to the value of satisfied and loyal customers. It takes far fewer retention dollars to increase the amount of business done with a current customer, than acquisition dollars to find and sell to a new one.

To create customer interest, my business must fill an existing need in a creative and innovative way, or create a new want among customers. This means that to be successful, you don't necessarily have to reinvent the wheel. In most cases there is plenty of market for whatever product or service you have in mind, whether it is something new or something old done in a new way. What you need to do is decide who your target customers are going to be and then make an effort to build a market share that will support your business and generate a profit.

I am, and always will be, in the people business. I must consider people as my top priority, both as customers and employees. In order to recruit and keep quality people, I must pay fairly and provide an entrepreneurial-friendly environment for them to work in. Make sure that people who put their faith in you have that faith rewarded.

To remain profitable, I must look for ways to improve my efficiency and maximize the return on my time and financial resources. One of the challenges small business always faces is getting past the practice of trickle down economics. Trickle down is longing and hoping that some of the money from the top will eventually trickle down to the bottom line. Everyone in small business can tell you all too well about the thrill of sales and the agony of no profits.

I need to consistently look for efficient and effective methods to use to advertise and market my business. Most of us don't have the budget to apply the tried and true marketing formulas used by big business. Big bucks are needed to create a business profile and top-of-mind awareness in the marketplace. In the beginning, my advice is that you use the best and cheapest marketing tool at your disposal: YOU. Get out and talk to as many potential customers as you can, and at the end of the day, when you think you can't possibly make another call, make just one more. By doing this, you'll make an additional 200 calls a year to potential customers.

In order to stay in business, I need to control my expenses. A good way to begin the process of controlling your expenses is to identify the five major areas of your business that consistently use up most of your financial resources. Then review each of the areas, with the objective of reducing the expenditure in each area by 20 percent. You will be surprised at how quickly you can uncover ways to cut down on operating expenses using this simple exercise.

I have to operate my business with the understanding that there is no such thing as maintaining the status quo. I have to do everything I can to generate continuous and manageable growth, or my business will go into decline. Your business is like a living organism. It can only ever be in one of two stages, either growing or dying. In business, as in nature, there is no such thing as staying the same. Cheryl, I know you know all this already, but it never hurts to step back from the trees once in a while to make sure we can still see the entire forest.

I'm also going to recommend, you keep reviewing the other aspects of your business to ensure you're giving enough thought to generating more sales, and particularly more profitable sales.

Give some thought to the following:
1. The quantity of potential customers you are contacting. Do you have realistic objectives for the number of daily, weekly and monthly sales calls you plan to make?

2. The quality of the potential customers you contact. Have you given enough thought to the specific market sectors most likely to respond to your services? Have you put together a 'most likely customer profile' to help you narrow your focus?

3. The methods you're going to use to make contact with your potential customers. Are you continuing to monitor and review the results you're getting from personal calls, telemarketing, direct mail, or fax? Have you designed tandem formats, using one method for initial contact and a second for follow up?

4. Your effectiveness in both one-on-one and group sales situations. You know the services you provide inside out, but are you able to explain them to your customers in simple, 'what's in it for them' terms? Do you have some visual material in your sales presentation? Are you closing each presentation with a simple request for an order? Can you justify your price in terms of the quality of your service and the benefits to your customer, when price is an issue?

Doug

OFF TO A SLOW START

Dear Doug,

Tried calling you on the week-end a few times. I guess you were at the cottage. I know better than to call you there. Right now I feel like my business is some kind of mutant vacuum, sucking everything up and out instead of in. It sure would be nice to see my company name on a significant contract right about now. I'm beginning to wonder if I will still remember how to spell sales or profit.

I'm taking your advice to heart and maintaining my focus on my business plan, but I would be less than honest if I didn't admit that my focus is pretty fuzzy at times. I'm still putting in the time and effort to make contact with potential customers who fit my target market profile, but it is really tough sledding. I sure would like to see some of that trickling down you referred to begin soon. Actually, I have made some solid contacts and one of them is through the regional office of my former company. You probably remember Ron Wallace one of the product managers, he called me last week to catch up on how things are going and said he was going to refer me to a friend, and he did. I followed up on the referral and I have an appointment to meet with him next week. All in all, I'm hanging on to my optimism, but my grip slips from time to time. Sometimes at the end of what seems to be another treading-water day my confidence button could use a little polishing. The lost and lonely feelings seem to kick-in right about the time I close my eyes and try to get to sleep. It is right about then that the self-doubt ogre appears and begins his nightly dance inside my head. I sometimes feel like I'm drowning in my own anxiety. I go over and over in my mind what I might be doing wrong, or what I should be doing that I'm not. I know we spend a lot of time on the phone going back and forth on the subject of staying positive but in spite of our combined efforts I have to admit that these days at least once every day, the thought flashes through my mind: do I really have what it takes? I think you can get an idea by the mood swings in this letter that the highs are getting lower and the downs are getting deeper.

Cheryl

There are occasional moments for everyone when we are free from worry... these brief moments we call panic!

HINTS FROM
SUCCESSFUL ENTREPRENEURS

Dear Cheryl,

    You're right we do spend a lot of time talking you up when you get down, but it goes with the territory. It's part of the mentor's manifesto. Your question to yourself, "Do I really have what it takes?" is one that will continue to haunt you off and on until you reach the goals you've set for yourself. You are a results oriented person and all the coaching and coaxing that I do isn't going to make the doubt go away, but the results you are going to achieve will. Actually, I think I'll lob the ball back into your court and ask: do you believe you have what it takes? It doesn't much matter what I, or anyone else thinks, what matters is what you believe. And by the way, your question is a little late isn't it? You're in now and you are either going to sink or swim to the other side. There's no turning back.

    I thought it might help you to hear what some others who have gone through the same start-up experience had to say about it. So I took the time to ask a few people, whose business competence I respect, to tell me what traits or characteristics had helped them through the early years and to achieve their success. One person told me that business competence was the result of mixing together equal amounts of book smarts and street smarts. While I listened to him, I was reminded of what Albert Einstein said when asked about learning and education, "I couldn't wait to get finished with my formal education so I could start learning" was his reply. My friend summed it up by saying he never expected to have every answer, but he never expected to encounter every problem either.

Another business associate told me she thought it was important to be consistent in her thoughts and actions when dealing with employees, customers and herself.

A third felt that motivating people by example and encouragement was what had made her successful. She also felt it was helpful to be willing to communicate openly and candidly with people, whether they agreed or disagreed with her outlook.

Having, as he put it, the courage to pose tough questions and accept straight answers was something a friend of mine felt had stood him in good stead over the years.

One very successful business woman I have known for the five years she has operated her business believed a gentle and self-deprecating sense of humor had helped her through many a crisis. As she so aptly explained, she takes what she does, not who she is, very seriously.

One man told me that the ability to think creatively and have the courage to make changes to even the most successful aspects of his business were important characteristics.

A very successful businessman I have had the good fortune to know for over 20 years told me he is still working on improving his weaknesses and shortcomings. He said he really never expects to complete the task, but the challenge helps keep him young and the project has taken him down paths over the years that he might not have otherwise considered. He also suggested it was important that he didn't expect to be right all the time and he did not beat up on himself when he was wrong.

The last person I talked to suggested it is important to encourage everyone in your organization to offer solutions when pointing out problems.

My own contributions would be these; I think one of the common characteristics of all the people I talked to is, they are self confident and comfortable with who they are, what they do and how they do it. They have all worked at conquering or coping with their own shortcomings. The result, that I can see, is these are people who can be, and enjoy being, themselves. I also believe positive thoughts create destinations, positive actions keep you on course during the journey and positive attitude makes getting there more fun. Remember, life is like a mirror, it will reflect back to the thinker what is thought into it.

Doug

Advice is what we ask for when we already know the answer but wish we didn't!

MAKING   DECISIONS

Dear Cheryl,

Interesting comment you made about making decisions, during our phone conversation last week. I think anyone running a small business can relate to the way you're feeling. Your reference to being tired at the end of the day from just making decisions would be funny, if it weren't so true. When you run a small business, you need big shoulders. Atlas had it easy, it would seem, in comparison to your average small business entrepreneur. All he had to do, was carry the weight of the world on his shoulders. As every small business entrepreneur can tell you, that's an insignificant task compared to carrying the weight of one small business. Its so important to try to make the right decision the first time because it can be very expensive to be in the 'let's try it again' business. I've always thought small business was a bit like marriage in that regard.

I think one of the most obvious, but often overlooked skills small business people need is the ability to make decisions, and make them right the first time. When you get knee deep in the everyday operations of a small business, you also get up to your eyeballs in making decisions. Sometimes it gets to the point where you begin to think, what you really went into was the decision making business.

In the early stages of your business, you can categorize your decisions this way: some decisions are very significant, some are less significant, but none are insignificant. The first, and most obvious factor in making decisions of any kind, is to be willing to make them. This isn't quite as simple as it sounds. Most day-to-day administrative decisions, unless you are starting your own nuclear reactor, will likely fall into the less significant category. Ignore them at your own peril however, because they can easily grow like a fungus, blanketing and suffocating the life out of your business. Don't let them pile up on you. Set up an early morning, let's-get-it-over-with time, to get them off your desk and out of your life. Eventually, your business will grow to the point where you can afford a detail doctor, more commonly referred to as an administrator.

The decisions falling into the significant category almost always come with an option you didn't order - additional stress. You'll find throughout the lifetime of your business, you'll be faced with the dual combination of the significant decision and the build-up of stress. One rule you can count on pertaining to the making of decisions in small business is, the more significant the decision, the higher the level of stress that will accompany it. The stress created, makes it that much harder to make the right decision. It's important that you balance the time and energy you put into making a decision, against the significance of it.

Try not to make any critical decisions in the heat of battle. Take time to hunker down in your bunker, regroup, calm down and gather your thoughts, so you can be more certain of making the right decision.

When called on to make a decision with critical or long term implications to your business, do your homework first. Review every option available to you, carefully and objectively. Stay objective and focus on facts. Save your emotional thoughts and outbursts for the next meeting of your sensitivity group, or your next rant. Gather the facts you need, get some informed opinions and collect other data you need by reading, listening and consulting. Look at the likely results of your decision from the perspective of everyone who will be affected. This isn't the time to gather your support group together and have them agree with everything you are thinking and saying. This is the time to seek diversity of opinion. Remember though, the game is played on your court, how the game is played will be your decision.

When making decisions, beware the dreaded paralysis by analysis. If you want to make a singular problem multiply, think too much and do too little. Once you're satisfied you've thought a situation through and you've considered all the information available to you, get on with making the decision. You're never going to please all of the people even most of the time. Your responsibility as a business owner is to make the decision and live with it. The obligation of people working with you, is to accept the decision and work with it.

One more small thing, when it comes to making decisions, don't discount intuition. Sometimes, in spite of the data you've gathered, the opinions you've sought, and the thinking you've done, it's best to follow your instincts. 'Ready, aim, fire' or 'ready, fire, aim', I guess it's your decision.

Doug

You probably wouldn't worry so much about what people think of you, if you knew how seldom they do!

SELLING ISN'T SO EASY

Dear Doug,

It would appear that of all the things I am, none of them is a salesperson. What am I doing wrong? I thought anybody could be a salesperson. I thought it was what you did when you ran out of things to do. But my appreciation for the skills required to make a sale increases ten fold every time I try to make one and I fail. I took your earlier advice and bought some books to help me improve my selling skills. I'm also enrolled in an eight week evening course on selling skills that begins in two weeks. I find the hardest part of the selling process so far is having to make telephone calls to prospective customers. I actually get nervous and anxious when I sit down to make them. I get myself ready to make calls and then back away at the last minute. When I do work up the courage to call, I usually end up having to leave a voice mail message. Oh, how I used to love voice mail when I was inside looking out, and how I hate it now, when I'm on the outside trying to get in. When I do get through to someone, I don't have much luck getting them to agree to meet with me. I have a valuable and needed service to offer to customers, but at this point I seem to be the only one who knows it.

When a prospective customer begins to ask me about my service, I immediately launch into some rambling, disjointed and mega-fast explanation about why I think they should do business with me. I catch myself in the middle of these mile a minute sales pitches sometimes and I can almost hear the panic in my voice. My telephone technique is obviously ineffectual and needs improving in both what I say, and the way I way it. Ironically I feel relaxed and confident in front of prospective customers during the few face to face meetings I'm able to generate. I'm even relaxed and enjoy doing group presentations. It's the phone that panics me, it seems to be some kind of evil device that scrambles my mind, dries up my throat and opens my sweat glands the minute I pick it up.

I need to take back everything negative I ever said about salespeople. They are definitely not the 'great unskilled' as I used to refer to them. Any thoughts on how I might become more productive while wearing my salesperson hat? Why is it so difficult just to make the calls? How do I get my foot and the rest of me in the door? Your comments and suggestions are invited and will be gratefully received. The good news is I'm continuing to get referred to people out here by people back there. So far those are the bulk of the appointments I've generated.

Cheryl

PROSPECTING FOR
NEW CUSTOMERS

Dear Cheryl,

So you're finding out that professional sales isn't as easy as you thought it would be. Yes - it's difficult for someone with no sales experience to put a shine on their shoes, a smile on their face and sell, sell, sell. In fact, I think a lot of small businesses fail within their first or second year not because they are under capitalized, but because they are under sold. What I mean is they fail because of ineffective selling by the sales staff, which in most cases is YOU. Your questions and comments about your selling skills, or lack of them, reminds me, we haven't really ventured too far down that road yet. A couple of weeks ago, I was asked by a group of sales professionals, to put together a talk on how to generate selling opportunities. You might pick up some ideas from the notes I've included in this letter.

First of all, let's tell it like it is. I don't know of anyone in sales who jumps out of bed in the morning and yells, "Thank you, God, for another chance to do more sales prospecting." There's a price to be paid in order to be successful in any business and sales prospecting is the price anyone in direct sales, or operating a business that is sales-driven, pays to be successful.

I like to ask small business owners, what they like most about selling and what they like least. The answer I get a lot really offers an insight into why I think sales professionals deserve and should be given a lot more respect for the job they do. A lot of business owners tell me they like having the opportunity to sit down with someone and make a sale. What they don't enjoy is having to do what needs to be done to bring about the opportunity. Bottom line, they don't like prospecting for sales.

Sales prospecting is simply making contact with people who are not yet your customers, for the purpose of giving them the opportunity to say yes, no or maybe. Your objective when prospecting is to uncover potential customers who have either a need for your product or service now, or who could be expected to have a need in the near future.

Try using this simple three part formula and see if the results of your sales prospecting improve. First make sure you're comfortable making sales prospecting calls. The best way to do it is to be yourself, don't try to learn some word for word canned sales pitch, it isn't you and it won't work. People know you're a one woman operation, why not tell them sales is not your specialty but creative design is, most people will respect your honesty and give you a chance. People today don't need to be sold, as much as they need to be given a 'what's in it for me' reason to buy.

Second, make sure especially in the start-up phase of your business that you put in the time and make the effort to prospect for sales consistently. Make it your number one priority. Depending on what stage of development your business is in and what is being sold, you need to allocate anywhere from ten to twenty-five percent of your time to sales prospecting. Third, make sure you take time out to evaluate what you're doing and the results you're generating. You need to keep track of what's working for you and what isn't. The most unproductive thing you can do is to keep doing more of what isn't working. It's like going to another country, and trying to communicate with people when you don't speak their language and they don't speak yours. It doesn't do you much good to continue to speak English only louder and slower and expect people to understand you. You might speak to a lot of people but the results you get aren't going to be very satisfying. Evaluate all of your prospecting systems and techniques as you go and adjust what needs to be adjusted before the frustration level causes you to give up.

Consider the various methods available to you for making contact with prospective customers. Then consider how best to use those contact methods, either individually or in tandem, to generate the best results. For instance, making calls on customers in person generates the highest return per contact, but not if the personal call is made without having previously set up an appointment. Usually a combination of direct mail and telephone follow up is needed to generate the appointment you need to make your personal sales call most effective.

I'm not a believer in cookie-cutter prospecting. There are, however, some rules of thumb that apply in most cases. Direct mail can be used to cover wide geographic areas and takes less time than telemarketing. Direct mail can be used to create initial interest in something new. Most often, you will use the telephone either as an initial contact tool or as a follow-up to direct mail. Success in using the telephone to generate appointments is based on two factors: what you say and how you say it.

Some businesses, of course, contract out direct mail and telemarketing to companies providing that type of specialized service, but in the early start-up stages of most small businesses, it'll be you who'll be the director of direct mail, and the telemarketing tester. In other words, you're going to be the guy in the funny hat and the baggy pants leading the mule up the hill. Happy prospecting.

Whatever ways or means you decide to use for your sales prospecting the key will always be your willingness to 'make the calls'. Nothing gets sold unless someone gets out and sells it. So here's a little self analysis that will help you determine how willing or reluctant you are to do sales prospecting. Have some fun with it and be sure to complete it before you decide to order that 'world's greatest salesperson' plaque for yourself.

Just answer yes or no to the following questions and statements. If you answer yes too often your sales are suffering because you're avoiding making your calls by thinking too much and doing to little. You'll find the scoring key at the end of the letter.

1. I spend as much or more time planning to make sales calls as I do actually making them.
2. It's uncomfortable for me when I have to call someone I don't know and ask them for an appointment.

3. I haven't quite finished putting together my initial target list of people I want to call, but I'm working on it.

4. I would rather be a guest on Jerry Springer than do a sixty minutes of cold calling.

5. I would spend more time prospecting for new customers, if more pressing issues didn't take up so much of my time.

6. I have clear goals and objectives and I love to talk about them with anyone who will listen.

7. I really like to give myself some time to get "psyched up" before I start making sales calls, but sometimes the time I need takes up most of my day.

8. I'd rather go back to school and take a math course than do cold calls.

9. I spend a lot of my time thinking about new, different and very unique ways to approach new customers, and then I like to mull them over for a while before I take any action.

10. I know I'm really good at making a sale once I get in the door and I work long and hard at perfecting my sales presentation. Unfortunately that cuts into the time I have for making the calls to set up the presentations.

Scoring Key - Total Yes Answers

One - Three
Just keep doing whatever it is your doing. Do not stop to think about it or analyze it.

Four - Seven
You're thinking a little too much about everything and not doing enough about anything.

Eight or More
The good news is you're a true thinker. The bad news is you're going to have lots of time to think, because you won't be in business long.

Whenever you do get an opportunity to make a sales presentation, don't waste it. You've worked too hard and invested a lot of time and energy getting from your office to the customer's, make it count. Here's a little check list you can use to help you. Keep in mind that people tend to believe that the quality of the wrapping indicates the value of the content.

- Make sure you're well groomed. Neatness and cleanliness count, show respect for yourself and your customer.
- Are you dressed to suit the situation? Don't dress to overpower. Convey a friendly , relaxed, professional image.
- Clear your mind and concentrate, don't appear distracted.
- Never make rude or off-color comments and save your stand up comedy act for another time and place.
- Project a warm, friendly confidence in your product or service and your expertise.
- Give the impression of being positive and enthusiastic about what you say, by the way you say it.
- Give the impression of physically fit energy, even on the last call of the day.
- Try, as hard as it may be, to listen and respond as much as you initiate. In other words, try to coordinate the use of your eyes, ears and mouth.

There's no great mystery to making an effective sales presentation. The first thing you should do is forget you're making a sales presentation. I didn't say forget making them, what I mean is, don't think of them in those terms. Effective selling is more about having the ability to communicate in a positive, knowledgeable, non threatening way than about giving it the old 'razzle-dazzle selling pitch'.

Try thinking about your sales calls presentations as if you were a guest in someone's home for the first time. What would you do to ensure you are appreciated as a guest and receive an invitation back? You would probably start by concentrating on smiling and being friendly. You would comment favorably on the surroundings. You would engage your host in conversation that focused on topics of interest and relevant issues. You would ask and respond to conversational questions, in order to share information. A good productive sales call isn't much different. This perspective on conducting sales presentations should help you relax and enjoy making them.

That's it for now. More about selling in my next letter in a few weeks. Don't forget, nobody likes to prospect, but success will continue only if you are willing to do what needs to be done, when it needs doing.

Doug

Conditions are never just right. People who delay action until all conditions are favorable tend to spend a lot of time sitting!

CONFIDENCE BEGINS TO BUILD

Dear Doug,

Thanks, I think. Was your comment about dragging my mule up the hill a polite way to tell me to get my ass in gear? If it was, it worked. I have begun developing a sales prospecting system using your ideas as a guide. I have started to systematically send out direct mail teasers to select prospects and I intend to make follow-up phone calls within 10 days of sending out the piece. I will let you know how things turn out. I had a couple of meetings this week with some prospective customers and your advice on thinking of a sales call in terms of a making a social visit really helped me to relax. It helped me to structure my presentation and focus on getting the information I needed through conversational questions. It really helped everyone in the meeting get a very friendly and productive dialogue going.

On the personal front, I have made some friends here and have discovered some funky and affordable neighborhood pubs and eateries. A few of us get together most Friday nights for a little mind unwind. Our favorite local bistro is called "Forget It." By about 10 o'clock most of us have. Ever since Meighan became engaged she has dedicated herself to what is best described as a zealous crusade to find me "the right guy." Hey, she found me a great place to live, why not let her take up the next challenge. I'm really beginning to feel good about my new life here. When I go out, I don't feel like it's with new friends anymore, it's just with friends. When I get home I feel at home. I can feel my comfort level increasing and my confidence building. I have a re-kindled determination to make my business a success and I feel like I'm developing the patience needed to work in harmony with it. I don't feel like I'm pushing against it as much as I did. I feel like I've found the rhythm of working with it instead of at it. I feel more in control of what I can control and more tolerant and accepting of what I can't. I'm no longer so anxious to live in the future that I let the present slip by unnoticed and unappreciated. I have the strangest feeling that I am beginning to understand how to be successful as me and that success in my business will follow. I know there will still be forks in the road, but I also sense that some unerring compass will guide me to choose the right path. This will sound really odd, but I feel braver and that there is much less to be afraid of. For the first time in my life, I am driven to accomplish all that I can, but to be satisfied with all that I am. I think I'm getting to know who I am, and that the person I am is good at what she does, and getting better. I guess I could sum it up this way, I've come face to face with risk, I understand it and I respect it, but now I know how to deal with it, and I have no fear of it.

Cheryl

THE SALE IS NEVER COMPLETE

Dear Cheryl,

I'm going to set your last letter aside and send it back to you the next time you start giving yourself a hard time. It was a very insightful, interesting and I thought, upbeat letter to read. I'm sure it took some doing to get the words down on paper. I told you it wouldn't take long for you to find new friends and fit into the new lifestyle you are putting together for yourself. I appreciate the fact that you feel comfortable enough with me to share some very personal feelings. You really put the risk reward teeter-totter that all entrepreneurs play on in perspective. You've accepted the risk and I'm sure if you continue to put in the hours and put out the effort the reward won't be too long in coming.

You asked me on the phone earlier in the week to continue with my thoughts on what makes a successful salesperson, so here they are. I'm going to offer a few additional random thoughts on selling, and then talk about the importance of staying in consistent contact with your customers and prospects.

It's not enough for you to know you have a valuable and beneficial service or product to offer. When all is said and done, you need to be able to convince others of the merits of your product or service. Today it has to be sold the right way. It is becoming more apparent that new ways of doing things call for new ways of selling things.

I find many new business owners who don't have any previous selling experience are embarrassed by the idea of having to become a salesperson. They think they are going to have to make themselves over into some kind of high pressure flim flam artist twisting the arms of the unsuspecting with 'if I've got it, you need it' high pressure selling.

That is not the case anymore. I see a new breed of salespeople today who are hardworking, creative, and put the needs of their customers and clients first. They are the ones who are prospering. In a conversation we had recently a friend of mine put it this way, she said; "I think the buying public still wants to buy as much as ever, but I don't think they react favorably to high pressure selling tactics." There is no doubt in my mind that educated consumers today are turning their collective backs on pressure tactics, they want to make an informed buying decision with the help of knowledgeable, empathetic salespeople.

Any business hoping to grow on repeat business and customer referrals has to put customer satisfaction first. For these enlightened businesses the sale is never complete. Staying in touch with your target market and customer base is a critical step in building any business. As you build your business contacts, you should begin to develop a stay-in-touch system.

Your stay-in-touch system is based on a constantly-expanding list of customers and prospects you contact periodically by using a combination of personal contact, direct mail and telephone contact. Your stay-in-touch list is really another component of your prospecting system and will be built, for the most part, on the results of your prospecting activities. You will find that when prospecting for customers you will uncover people with a near term need for your product or service, as well as people who have an interest but no near term need. The first group become your immediate target market and you take the appropriate steps to sell them on becoming customers. The latter group are added to your stay-in-touch list.

Systematically building and maintaining an active and profitable stay-in-touch list is easy.

1. Assemble an initial list from your prospecting activities.
2. Make an effort to add to the list consistently.
3. Record and file all customer and prospect information accurately.

4. Stay in touch with everyone on your list through a combination of mail, telephone or personal contact either monthly, quarterly or twice annually.

Like any system, you have to monitor the results to make sure you are getting a profitable return on the time and effort you are putting in. Evaluate your stay-in-touch results annually using format like this.

1. How many additions to my list have been generated this year?
2. How many sales have been generated from the prospects on my list?
3. How many referrals have been generated from current customers?
4. How many of those referrals have resulted in business?
5. Who should be deleted from the list?

That's it for now. Remember customers and prospects have short memories, don't let them forget you. Keep reminding them that you're ready, willing and able.

Doug

GET RID OF NEGATIVE BAGGAGE

Dear Cheryl,

Your recent email wondering what separates the winners from the also-rans in business, really struck a cord. I've been thinking about it ever since. I'm not really sure I or anyone else has the definitive answer. What separates the winners from the losers in small business? What separates the winners from the losers in anything? There are, of course, both tangible and intangible factors that enter the equation. Your chances for success are better if you are well-financed, but a lot of people with very deep pockets find that, in the end, the pockets aren't deep enough to make them successful. Your chances for success increase if you are dedicated to working as long and hard as it takes to be successful, but unfortunately, that's not a guarantee either. I know people who have worked harder than you and I would ever think possible, and still weren't successful. Like any good consultant, however, if I don't know the answer, I'll just throw as much mud on the wall as I can and hope some of it sticks. Stand back and try not to get splattered, here comes the mud.

Even though I don't think I have the answer, the experience I've gained over the last 10 years operating my little piece of the global economy has left me with some thoughts, opinions and observations about what separates winners and losers in the small business game. To begin with I don't believe, or at least I'm yet to see, any universally accepted definition of what a small business entrepreneur is. No one, it seems to me, has of yet accurately defined what a small business entrepreneur really is, although various benchmarks do exist. Some people judge a small business by number of employees, others on sales revenues. My own benchmark or definition is this; if you work full time in, and earn your primary income from, a business you own , you are a small business entrepreneur. In the media, there seems to be a tendency to paint what I consider 'micro businesses', and small businesses with the same brush. A micro-business operator is often really a business hobbyist.

For the micro-business entrepreneur, the focus is on additional, not primary income. While many of these people are creative and dedicated entrepreneurs, most are not interested in building their business into anything beyond something to generate additional lifestyle-enhancing income.

Let me digress for a minute and throw in a personal observation about the attitudes of people working in big versus small business. It has become apparent to me during my flirtations in and out of corporate America, that there is a kind of unspoken feeling of big is better held by a lot of people working in large companies. Let me use a baseball analogy to make my point. A lot of the people working in large companies or big business as it is referred to, mistakenly believe that by working in a large company they are playing in the business big leagues, while small business people toil in the minors. I grant you that it may be true that they are in the big leagues, but most are fringe players at best. The reality is that few if any really get into the game. I define a big league business player as someone who can and does make decisions that impact on the day-to-day and future development of the business - someone who sits at a desk where the buck stops. In spite of the empowerment rhetoric showing up in almost every edition of every big company newsletter, how many people in large companies can make decisions that affect the day to day and future operations of the company as a whole? How many really have any significant decision making powers? If you use decision making as a benchmark, then small business is the business big leagues and entrepreneurs are the players in it.

Small business is a game that demands, above all, emotional and mental strength. Not the strength you might associate with an oak tree that can withstand the onslaught of nature without bending or breaking, but the strength of a willow that is able to bend but won't break. Almost every entrepreneur I know has faced times of adversity, times that tested their emotional and mental strength to the breaking point. Those who were able to bend without breaking were the ones left standing.

What gave them the emotional and mental strength to carry on? What created the reserves they needed to stay the course where others would give up? They had a strong, secure self concept. Self concept includes three important ingredients: your self image or how you see yourself, your self ideal or how you would like to see yourself, and your self esteem or how much you like yourself. A strong self concept can give you drive, determination and the edge you need to make the difference between success and failure in your business. It can be the factor that most determines whether you become an average or above average entrepreneur. A secure self concept will make you more confident about who you are, where you are going and how to get there.

The exciting thing, however is that we can all develop the self concept we want to wear through life. None of us are given a self concept, or forced to stand in line and take the next one available. Your self concept is based on your life experiences: your fears, your doubts, your likes and dislikes, your opinions and ideas and values. In other words, life's stuff. If the stuff you've collected over the years is weighing you down, get rid of some. You're never stuck with stuff, you're the one who decides what you want to pile on your shoulders and lug around with you. Lighten your load from time to time by taking stock of the stuff you really need and throwing out the rest. Toss out the bad memories, bad attitudes, negative thoughts and feelings, and maybe even some of those depressing country music albums you dig out and play when you really want to drive up your misery level. Replace the stuff that wears you down with new stuff that will pick you up, and move you forward. The lighter your load the faster you can move toward your new goals and objectives.

Any retro-fit on your self concept has to begin with some renovation work on your self image. Let me emphasize, however, that what you need to do is renovation work, not demolition work. You can't just expect to blow up the old you and have a new you emerge unscathed from the ashes. Making quality, lasting changes to anything takes willingness to set out on an incremental journey, which requires both time and patience.

Both innies and outies are important. No, I'm not referring to the results of a recent survey on belly buttons. What I mean is that when you operate your own business the inner you is going to impact on the outer you more significantly than it might in a 'I've got a real job, let the other guy worry about it' situation. The inner you needs to understand and accept some basic truths. You can only take out what you put in. Your business will grow and prosper in direct proportion to how and how often you apply your skills. The only way you can build your business into the success you want it to be is by focusing on doing the things that are consistent with what you want to accomplish. It's no secret that there is a direct link between concentration and compensation. With the possible exception of politicians, we all know that thoughts precede actions. Thinking about positive actions and outcomes will help you figure out the actions you need to take to generate increased results. One of the laws of physics states; that for every action there is an equal and opposite reaction. The small business entrepreneur's law says that to generate positive results, you must first initiate positive actions.

If you aren't prepared to take actions to make it happen for you, the only alternative is to wait for it to happen to you. Let me ask you this though: When you wait to get smarter, does it happen? When you sit around and wait to lose weight, does it work? When you wait for your skills to improve, do they get better? When you wait for your self confidence to grow, does it? A quick reminder here, Cheryl, that there are those who make things happen, those who watch things happen and those who are always wondering what's happening. Successful entrepreneurs can't afford to watch or wonder.

You could count on luck, or simply being in the right place at the right time, but that means you had better be one of the really lucky ones who are able to figure out how to be in the right place, at the right time, a lot of the time. It's not a real sure-fire success formula for most of us.

I believe it takes a very special person to take up the challenges of business ownership. Very often it is the people who were the square pegs that big business kept trying to stuff into the round holes.

A lot of people decide early in their working lives to walk the entrepreneurial road. Some, like you, take the walk later, after walking the corporate plank first. But I have a feeling that once the initial shock of being sacrificed on the altar of downsizing, right-sizing, left-sizing or whatever euphemism big business is using to justify getting rid of people today, wears off, a lot of the people shown out the door are glad to be sprung from a life sentence of big business boredom. Its a bit like getting off the dizzying, mind-numbing, going-in-circles, merry go round, then climbing aboard the dazzling, and yes sometimes stomach-churning, up-and-down roller coaster. I believe a lot of people today see the colors of their lives being bleached out because of negative job-related stress. Their days begin to be measured by lighter or darker shades of gray. Kind of like living in Seattle in November.

Too many people with average jobs in average companies are living one *why* day after another. *Why* days are the ones when you wake up and your first thought is 'why me, why this, why that, why it, why them, why him, why her, why bother?' *Why* days are not particularly stimulating, unless you're a confirmed masochist. You know it's another *why* day when you wish it was tomorrow, yesterday, or anything but today.

I think you'll find, Cheryl, that entrepreneurs have fewer *why* days and more *my* days. The reason? The minute you become an entrepreneur, you cease to be average. There are successful entrepreneurs and there are unsuccessful entrepreneurs, but there are no average entrepreneurs. No shades of gray for you, instead your world is about to become blinding in its clarity. The colors are so bright it's like living in a rainbow on steroids. *My* days are even those days when you get up from your five hours of anxiety-ridden tossing and turning, and groggily realize you feel two days older than dirt. Then shuffle through the pile of sixty days overdue notices in your accounts payable file. And realize that if the day progresses as it should, you may have a chance to catch up enough to almost feel close to getting caught up on the things you planned to get done yesterday. It's right about then that you realize what having your own business is really about, and you still love it.

You realize that having your own business isn't about you or the business, it's about the spirituality of singular accomplishment. It's about the satisfaction of not simply knowing you're right, but of knowing it's right for you. You're not thinking about it, you're not dreaming about it, you're not wishing it were so - you're doing it. You are one of the people who decided to get up off the couch.

Doug

If you can't believe in yourself, you can't believe in success. The basis of your success will always be your faith in your own ability to succeed.

A DAY IN THE LIFE

Dear Doug,

Why days, or my days - interesting concept. I think I have mostly my days, but I sure stop to ask myself why, a lot of times during those days.

Let me take you through a day in my life, and you decide what kind of day you would call it. My day begins at 6:00 this morning. I'm into my new early morning exercise workout followed by my 20 minute walk rain or shine, with wrist weights firmly attached. I feel like Robo woman walking with those things on. This new exercise friendly me, probably means I'm becoming a real left-coaster. It's 7:30 and I'm at the desk in my office. I'm sipping the first of my daily 'way-to-many' cups of coffee. I find ideas for my design work seem to flow more freely early in the morning, so I try to get in at least an hour of creative work before the nuts and bolts part of the business day takes over.

It's now around 9:30 a.m., I'm sitting on a stool at my kitchen counter having another jolt of caffeine, reading yesterday's news and waiting for my breakfast to be served. Another day when no one shows up to fill that role, so I skillfully whip up a wholesome breakfast of frozen no-name waffles covered in delicious and nutritious wannabe maple syrup. I finish my bottomless cup of coffee and make another promise to myself to get into the fruit and fiber thing starting tomorrow.

It's around 10:00 and I begin working on the outline for a proposal

I'm presenting to a group building six new restaurants. Each is to have a different food theme and interior design. I'm also working for the first time on a proposal outside the hospitality industry. I have been asked to submit some interior design and decorating ideas for a medical services group who manage clinics throughout the northwest and into California. I am also putting the finishing touches on a proposal I'm presenting to a prospective client next week. The rest of the morning was a typical mix of phone calls in and out, paperwork, and work on some ideas for a new direct mail folder I am hoping to have ready for the printer by next week.

I love the challenge!

At 11:30 a.m. I get myself and my materials together, self taking most of the time. I'm heading for a lunch appointment with a colleague from my networking group and a prospective client he is introducing me to. The lunch went well, the prospective client and I are getting together for a second meeting next week.

It's now 2:15 p.m. and I'm waiting for a prospective client to free herself from a meeting so that we can begin our 2:00 meeting. I never know how long I should stay when someone makes me wait past a scheduled appointment. I finally got to sit down with my 2:00 appointment at 2:20. She was very apologetic, and I was very understanding, what else can you do? It's 3:40 p.m., I'm on my way to a specialty lighting supplier to check out what is available. Isn't gridlock wonderful, gives you all that time to listen to your in car CD collection, and try out your new 'I'm not going to get strung out over traffic attitude'. Well 6:15 and I'm back at world headquarters; the new attitude didn't work! I can feel myself going into my end of day fade, I need to crash for a twenty minute cat nap. I better just take a couple of minutes and check my voice mail first. O.K. all caught up and ready for that 20 minute nap, I wake up 45 minutes later.

I don't feel much like dinner now, think I'll just grab a chocolate bar and get a bit more work done. I'm back in the office putting together some emails and responding to a couple of others that I received today. It's now about 8:30p.m., I should break for dinner but I just want to put together a few charts and slides and make a few changes to my notes for a sales presentation I'm making on Friday. Does everyone who makes up slides and charts for presentations labor over them as long as I do? The perfectionist in me reared it's ugly head again tonight and I took over 90 minutes for a job that I'm sure anyone else could accomplish in 30. Done, but it's now after 10:00, and suddenly I'm starving.

I'm coping with the wait for my dinner by sipping a glass of wine while sitting in front of the babble box watching some very funny people perform on the comedy channel. No free dinner tonight, delivery in twenty eight minutes. It's now just after 11:00 p.m., hard to believe how fast an evening can slide by on you isn't it? That's it for this entrepreneur's day. A why day or a my day? What would I call it? I'm not sure, I'm too tired to think about it.

Cheryl

THE MONEY IS IN THE SOLUTIONS

Dear Cheryl,

    I still think it was a 'my' day. In this letter I want to expand on the topic we discussed on the phone last week, the ongoing problem - of problems. Yes, you will find unexpected problems are an almost daily challenge during the first 12 to 18 months of the development of your business. After that they don't go away, you just become a little smarter and able to anticipate them. Then they aren't able to sneak up and bite you as often. But do not despair - keep reminding yourself, the first 10 years are always the toughest. When you are the grand pooh-baah of your own business, you get to spend time you haven't got, handling problems you wish you didn't have. Oh, the joys of small business ownership. But enough with the needling and onto the suggestions.

    When operating any business you will find yourself faced almost continuously with problems that are created either through action or inaction. The important thing to remember is you don't make money by thinking about your problems, you make money by focusing on finding solutions to them. In other words, give the problems some thought, decide on actions designed to solve them and get on with it. Don't let skinny little problems become overweight issues by sitting too much and thinking, when you should be up and doing. While your actions may not be right every time, they won't be wrong all the time either. If you spend too much time focused on what went wrong, you'll sap the creative energy you need to focus on the more important issue of what is going right. I know you're going to get tired of me climbing on this same old horse, but here we go again.

You must work with an attitude that enables you to look at your problems and work out solutions to them. But you should also stand back now and then and look through your problems for the possible opportunities they may represent. Get in the habit after you solve a problem of asking yourself questions designed to uncover opportunities that may lie buried within them.

It's very important not to over think a problem. Thoughts can create perceptions which, good or bad, may limit how you deal with reality. Becoming obsessed with finding a perfect solution or course of action tends to enlarge the scope of the problem in your mind. This can lead to erecting more imaginary barriers to overcome and ultimately, can turn the proverbial mole hill into a mountain. Try using this formula to deal with problems. Recognize the problem, give it some thought, take some action, live with the results, move forward. By the way, Cheryl, while you're asking yourself all these questions, once in a while be sure to ask yourself this one. Am I having fun yet?

Doug

MARKETING STRATEGY

Dear Cheryl,

Just a short follow-up on our recent conversations about what you are doing to market your business and some additional thoughts on the differences between big and small business marketing and product and service marketing.

People have come to think of marketing in terms of the expensive, slick, multi-media campaigns we see used by the giants of the automobile, computer, and soft drink industries for example. Small business entrepreneurs are naturally restricted by somewhat smaller marketing budgets. Wouldn't it be nice to have a couple of hundred million, instead of a couple of hundred to spend on marketing. You need to think of marketing in terms of any activity that takes your service or product from you to your client.

Marketing for most small business people consists of two components advertising, and direct sales, or the way I think of it is, getting your name out, and taking yourself out. There is, subtle but significant difference between marketing most products compared to most services. Most elements of advertising like print media, radio, television, and direct mail, have a higher rate of return when used to promote a product than they do when promoting a service. A service provider especially during start-up must almost always place more emphasis on directly selling his or her service. That means good old fashioned personal telephone calling and door knocking.

When customers are buying a service they can't see it, or touch it. Buying a service means taking a leap of faith. A customer has to believe the service provider is going to do what they say they will. The whole exercise is one of perceived future value, so service marketing is really a process of helping your customers place a value on your service. You should think of service marketing in terms of things you do every day to help your customers appreciate and value what you do and how you do it.

Your advertising and personal selling efforts should be used to consistently create and reinforce a value perception in the minds of your customers. Marketing is a battle of perception and it's been proven that what the mind perceives, is what a person believes. Because perception is such an integral part of service marketing, and perception is more about feelings and emotions and less about facts, time is of the essence. If you take too long to make an impression with someone, that impression can become shrouded in feelings of doubt, negativity, ambivalence or apathy. Part of both your advertising and direct sales efforts should include a call to action. You must be able to explain to the customer how they will benefit by taking action now, and how they will benefit by taking it with you.

Whatever methods you decide to use in marketing your service, what really matters is that you develop a marketing strategy aimed at the heart of customer satisfaction. The most powerful, effective and elusive marketing tool, is what everyone refers to as "word of mouth advertising," and it can only be built one satisfied customer at a time. Any print advertising your use must be carefully thought out, both in terms of what is most likely to turn customers on, and what might turn them off. If you're trying to create long term customer relationships, don't promise what you can't deliver. Remember, when marketing a small business the only way to replace the dollars you don't have is with creativity, ingenuity and personal effort.

SUFFERING THROUGH
A SLOW START

Dear Doug,

A couple of months ago I wrote about how good I was feeling about my new life and how my confidence was growing. Forget it! Is it possible to be a positive-worrier? The good news is - I'm getting more chances to make proposals to prospective customers. In the past two months I've put together nine proposals. The bad news is - so far the score is proposals nine, business three. These were great proposals. I did my research and homework. I understood the customer's needs and wants. I took the time to double and triple-check my numbers. I put every ounce of creativity I could into each one. Some of them should have been the door opener into the hotel dining room design market I'm trying to get into, but none of those were accepted. The three that were accepted are for single owner operated restaurants. Don't misunderstand I'm grateful for the work, but some of the proposals I worked on had the potential to get me a contract with hotel chains that would help me build the type of reputation I need. I went against your advice and shaved my profit on the last two to just about the break-even point. Still nothing. What am I doing wrong?

I'm so tired at the end of every week. I can't seem to unwind and the thoughts of what I could have done differently or better seem to haunt me day and night. I'm becoming a recluse. I don't want to inflict myself on my friends when I'm like this. All I can think about is: what if I just don't have it? Right now my business is a job to job scramble, with limited revenue coming in, and no margin for error. What if my business remains that way? What if it just limps along generating just enough revenue and hope to keep it and me going? What if running my business turns out to mean running on empty? I don't think having the freedom to be my own boss, will be much fun, if I can't make enough money to pay the boss what she's worth.

Right now cash flow is getting a little tight. I'm still on target for expenses, but the projected revenue isn't there. Projections and reality sure look different on paper. When I put the numbers together in the projections, even the worst case start-up scenario didn't look too bad. But when I see the numbers on my monthly business statement, the reality of how close I am to using up all my start-up capital begins to sink in. In my heart of hearts, I really believed I would buck the odds and get off to a fast start, I guess everyone does. I understand you have to crawl before you can walk and walk before you run, but I feel like I'm stuck in the sitting up stage.

I'm really tempted to take some time off and regroup, but that's not really an option because of the projects I'm working on. I'm a little afraid to do it anyway because I feel like it's the big cop-out beckoning to me. I'm not even sure that if I stopped I would have it in me to re-start. I'm scared for the first time since I started. I've had a few minor

Sometimes I lie awake at night and ask; "Why me?" Then a voice answers, "Nothing personal your name just happend to come up."

failures in my thirty years, but I can't let this be one.

I'm glad I decided to put this letter aside for a couple of weeks before sending it. I've done some real soul searching since writing the first part. I've come to the conclusion that in spite of the contradiction in terms, I'm a positive - worrier. Deep down inside I'm still positive that I can make this business work. I'm just worried that I will run out of money before my efforts pay off. I seem to be in a period of time and state of mind, when the initial excitement of start-up has worn off and the reality of working at it and living inside it, is setting in.

I've decided my best course of action is to stop worrying about what might happen and focus all of my energies on what is. I re-examined my work pattern and I've decided there is nothing wrong with what I'm doing but I need to improve how I'm doing it. I'm working on two more significant proposals and I'm going to use a different format for both the written and visual components. I'm going to take a lot of the fluff and filler out of the written part and stick to what's in it for the customer in simple easy to measure terms. I'm going to shorten the visual part of the presentation and give it more visual impact by using more computer generated graphics in my slides. I even went back to a company that turned down one of my previous proposals and asked them for an opportunity to re-submit, and they have agreed to let me. My positive side is kicking in and I think if I stay the course, and learn to work a little smarter my efforts will pay off.

Cheryl

SMALL BUSINESS FLEXIBILITY

Dear Cheryl,

A positive-worrier, a funny but apt description I would say. You made a comment during a phone call about six weeks ago, and I think in light of your recent letter, now would be a good time for me to respond to it. You said that you felt like you burden me too much with your problems. First, the problems we discuss are never frivolous and therefore they are not a burden. I enjoy being a sounding board for what goes on both good and bad. Second it seems to me, more often than not, you ultimately solve the problem yourself after we talk it out. Finally let me remind you, almost every conversation we have has it's fair share of laughter. That's one of the things I like most about you, your strange and twisted sense of humor, the way you are able to see the absurdity in a lot of what goes on around us.

I really think you're being a little rough on yourself and that you've been demanding more of yourself than you should these past few months. Nobody, with the possible exception of Kathie Lee, is positive every minute of every day. I know this will come as a shock to you but you aren't Super-Lady. All right, close maybe, but you're still human and you will have some down days and doubts from time to time.

Don't get strung out over not having the answer to everything all the time. Some of your frustration is due, no doubt, to having spent all of your working life in a large organization, where most of your answers were preordained because of policies and procedures. Big business has a need for policies and procedures, but the only policy you should have at this point is to have no policy. The only procedure you need right now is to treat each of your customers as individuals.

If it means more questions you don't have a stock answer for, or dealing with situations you don't have a procedure in place to handle, go with it, so be it. Turn your willingness to be flexible when responding to your customer's needs and requests into a sales advantage.

Leave it to the big guys to be governed by their policies and procedures, they can afford the fall-out. I'm not sure I ever told you my story about going to two banks to get a start-up loan for a business, many years ago. In both instances I was told my application did not meet lending policy. O.K. I thought, maybe I can make some changes and meet their policy. But, when I asked what the policy was, neither of the lenders could actually tell me what it was. What they had been told was to simply give me the answer, and the answer was, I didn't fit their policy. Now, if you want to talk frustration, try that one. I don't mind an occasional no, and I learned how to deal with rejection at my high school dances. But when someone rejects you, it's nice to know why.

I suggest you put up with your feelings of frustration and guard your flexibility with a passion. It's one of the great advantages you have over policy-bound big business.

I also think some of your frustration comes from not being able to be better at some of the things you have to do.

That's part of the curse of running your own business. You aren't operating in a departmentalized bubble like you were in your previous career. You were the definitive expert in your department, acknowledged master of your domain. You, like the other company specialists, were very good at what you did. But what you had to be very good at, was very limited. You were one of a team of specialists, your focus was defined and narrowed by your responsibilities.

Now your expertise has to cover a lot of ground and your focus has to cover a much broader range of tasks. You are out of necessity becoming a business generalist, a jack of all trades, and master of but a few. When you look at your business you see everything the good, the bad and the ugly, because it's your frog…warts and all. You'll have to remind yourself now and then that things may get a little messy and your hands may get a little dirty but what you're building belongs to you. For an entrepreneur that's enough.

You're probably getting a little physically tired at this stage of the game and that's bound to shorten your fuse and bump up your frustration level. Take a little of your time and make it 'your' time. Remember, if you think you're frustrated now, think about the last time you went to get the thing you put in the special place, so you wouldn't forget where it was. You know the place you put it so you'd know exactly where to go to get it, when you needed it.

Doug

Only the mediocre are always at their best, but their best isn't worth being at!

STOP FEELING SMALL

Dear Cheryl,

A few more thoughts in response to your positive-worrier letter. Over time, you've probably noticed that I am fond of comparing a small business entrepreneur's life to a ride on a roller coaster, even though I'm a confirmed coward when it comes to actually getting on one. You are going to have ups and downs, teasingly slow climbs up, sometimes followed by mind numbing stomach churning plunges into depths of despair. Then just as quickly rocketing forward and up again to new more exhilarating heights.

It looks like the game has truly begun. Increased numbers of proposals being generated, a few, but apparently not enough, being accepted. Remember when you would have sold your soul just for the chance to submit a proposal? How quickly our perspective can change. At this stage of the game it will seem as though each proposal you make carries with it the potential to make you or break you. In the early going, because you are your business, it is inevitable that you will feel the wounds of rejection more deeply. In the beginning, every proposal you make to a prospective customer will carry a big piece of you with it on the pages. Each proposal you make is magnified in importance. Each one is almost intimidating in its enormity. Each one takes on a life of its own and like the roller coaster ride it holds the capacity to take you to great heights or plunge you to great depths, depending on its success or failure.

Each one that is rejected hurts. It hurts more personally than it should, or than makes sense, but that doesn't make it hurt any less or the pain go away any sooner. Everyone can tell you there is nothing personal in the rejection, that it's just part of the game you've chosen to play. But when you're driven to win and you feel yourself losing, all of the stay positive commiserating from well meaning friends and supporters just begins to wear a little thin. You're already trying with every ounce of mental and emotional strength you possess to hold on to positive thoughts and images. In spite of your best efforts, sometimes you'll have moments when emotional, mental and physical fatigue will roll over you like a cold damp fog, shrouding you in doubt and self pity. When it happens your bright positive resolve can quickly dissolve into pools of dark negativity. There is no way for any of us to avoid an occasional bout with despair, nor should we necessarily want to. If we had no downs, we wouldn't know how good up can feel.

One more thing before I get on with my letter and off of your case. The magnitude of any single proposal is directly proportional to the number being worked on, and the amount of business you have. Over time, as you build your customer base and your business increases, each new proposal will be seen in its proper perspective as an opportunity to do some business, no more, no less.

Don't be too concerned about being a little slow getting off the ground at this point. You're still really in test flight mode. You've done your homework, you know the market is there for your service. You've picked up a few small jobs and it sounds like you are putting together more proposals every month. You know you're willing to make the effort and you have the talent. Keep in mind, you're not in the commodity business, yours is a specialty service geared to a niche market. As you said yourself, and my Ford and I resent it, you aren't selling low end-services - you want to be the Ferrari of commercial interior design. You knew going in that you would be faced with the entrepreneurs classic catch 22 dilemma. How do you prove your worth when people are hesitant to give you a chance? You know the answer - you just keep on, keeping on.

Let me ask you this, is your business really slower getting off the mark than you thought it would be or is it just slower than you want it to be? What really counts is whether you are on target to meet the first-year projections you made in your business plan. I suspect you are, but that you're already bored with the target you set. I doubt things are really developing at the snail's pace you describe. In fact they seem to be developing at about the pace you projected in your business plan. The only difference that I can see is that your business is coming from more small projects and fewer big ones, and that I might add isn't always bad. The big guys just haven't yet recognized your talents the way you were hoping they would. In the mean time use the opportunities your smaller clients have given you to develop your talent and style. Don't forget the power of word of mouth advertising, and testimonials from satisfied customers.

Start walking tall.

You're even sounding recently like you're starting to enjoy the selling part of the game. Isn't that an amazing growth step! Remember how hard you worked to convince yourself you would like everything about your business except the sales part? You know, it pains me to say, "I told you so," but I do seem to have a vague recollection of telling you that making sales calls could and would be relatively pain free.

Remember, even the most researched and well-documented business plan can sometimes spin a little out of control during the test flight of any business. Don't forget that until you get your business off the ground, there is no real way to tell how well it will fly. If you think you've got something to worry about, imagine how Neil Armstrong must have felt going to the moon and setting down in a lunar lander that he had crashed once in testing, and that he could never really get to stabilize perfectly during his test flights. He just knew that the mission might not be perfect but it was do-able. So far your mission may not be perfect, but it certainly isn't in danger of crashing and it is do-able. I'm not going to give you a verbal kick in the butt yet, but get your focus back on track before I have to ask whether you want a little cheese to go with your whine.

It sounds to me, when you dashed off your letter, you might have been having one of those down days we can all encounter every now and then. As I've said so many time over the years, it isn't easy to stay positive in a world that seems intent on surrounding us with unrelenting negativity. You'll snap out of any funk you get yourself in. You have all the reserves of determination you need to step around, through or over any negativity that stands in your way.

It may be true as you say, that you are one person struggling to turn the dream of a successful small business into a reality. But you have an awful lot of people to keep you company. Millions of small business entrepreneurs the world over are committed to the same struggle. Sometimes I think you and every other small business entrepreneur sometimes get to feeling like you're the smallest pea in the big economic pod. You couldn't be more wrong. Stop feeling small and start walking tall. You and your business are important. You're part of the fastest growing employment sector in the economy. As your business grows, you're going to become one of a very special group of people. You're going to become the owner of a business that creates employment and opportunity. What greater satisfaction could you want than that. Remember the old adage: give someone a fish and you feed them for a day, teach them to fish and you feed them for a lifetime. Before long Cheryl, you're going to be teaching some people to fish.

Doug

RAINY DAY SUNDAYS

Dear Doug

Glad you were able to track me down over the week-end. I know you weren't too surprised when I told you it was a rainy afternoon in Seattle. (No, it does not rain all the time in fact it doesn't rain most of the time, all right, all right it does rain a lot of the time). I really enjoyed the time we spent together on the phone. It sounds like you have a very full plate right now and again let me say how much I appreciate the time you take to offer your help to me. As I said, I feel like I'm getting close to getting that first big contract that I'm working so hard for. I have a number of proposals in the hopper and I'm hoping to hear from a couple of the companies within the next eight to ten weeks.

I'm enjoying my work with the small clients I have. I feel like the work I'm doing with them is building both my confidence and expertise. I really feel the experience gained working with them will help me when I get to work with larger accounts. My client list is continuing to grow and the really exciting thing for me is that a lot of my business is now coming through referrals from satisfied customers. Just this week I got a small redecorating job from a friend of a customer I had worked with recently.

I went out with some friends after our talk, and the conversation as always turned to business. It's one of the two things we talk about most often, I won't tell you what the other is. A few of them are small business service providers like me, and one of them tossed out an interesting question. He was wondering if the rest of us had any thoughts on whether people are likely to use the same decision making process when purchasing a service, as they do when purchasing a product. The group seemed equally divided between the 'a purchase is a purchase' group of which I was one, and the 'people make service and product purchase decisions' differently group. When you have a chance, I would like to get your thoughts on it. I'm going to call you next week to talk about some other things, maybe we can bounce it around then.

Cheryl

Strange how many people plan to live forever, and yet can't figure out what to do on a rainy Sunday afternoon!

WHY DOES A CUSTOMER BUY?

Dear Cheryl,

I'm glad you were picking up the tab for our phone conversation last week. I agree that letters, faxes and email have their place, but nothing in the communications equation beats a good animated conversation between two intellectual giants like us. In spite of the two hours spent on the phone, I think we still have some unfinished business. Sounds pretty ominous, doesn't it? Relax, I just got to thinking about my explanation about the difference between service and product buyers and what influences their buying decisions, and I decided to expand on my thoughts. Isn't this great? Now you don't even have to solicit my advice, you're getting it whether you need it or not.

Are people likely to use the same decision-making process when purchasing a service as they would purchasing a product? Do buying motives differ between service and product purchases? Why not just ask, why is the sky blue? As always though, I have an answer, thought, opinion, or ramble at the ready. So here it goes.

When buying a product, you buy something tangible. What you see is what you get. When buying a service, you are buying an intangible. What you can't see is what you are going to get. Chances are, if you like a product, or it captures your imagination, or you need it badly enough, you're going to part with the bucks and buy it. The person selling it matters, but not much. Whether or not you like the person selling the product, whether they are knowledge or personality challenged won't matter if your need for or fascination with the product is strong enough. You can if need be see over, under, through or around the person selling the product to the product itself. You can see, hear, touch, taste or smell the product. It's there in front of you, you can see if it works, or test drive it. When you buy a product it can be returned, or simply stored away for a couple of years and brought out for the next yard sale.

When buying a service the value factors most often associated with the purchase are saving time, lessening stress, increasing knowledge, or any combination of the three. You rarely buy a service on impulse or from a point of purchase display. You may, from time to time, have an overwhelming urge to buy a new pair of shoes or upgrade your blender, and throwing all caution to the wind, you often run out and do it. It's not too often however, that you buy accounting services just because you feel in a crazy mood and think it will be fun. In most cases, the decision to buy a service is more complex than the decision to buy a product. In most cases people want to be comfortable with and like the person they are purchasing a service from. The need for client - service provider comfort increases when the nature of the service is such that clients work closely with the service provider.

The three most common needs, service providers are called on to fill, are economy needs, efficiency needs and the need for excellence. It would seem then that selling a service is pretty simple, right? All you have to do is fill the customer's need for economy, efficiency and excellence, while offering them the value associated with saving time, decreasing stress and increasing knowledge. Not simple, and not easy. The fact is it's possible to deliver the three value factors associated with time, stress and knowledge, but it's not possible for you to fill the three E's of economy, efficiency and excellence, and still make a profit.

Coming to grips with imperfection is never easy, just ask me. But the sooner you accept the fact that nobody can provide economy, efficiency and excellence and still stay in business, the happier you and your customers will be. Allow me to give you an example of why you will be unable to deliver on the three E's. Let's say I am in the business of conducting seminars. I know, what an odd example for me to use. I can provide excellence in my seminars by providing personal attention, extensive and expensive course notes and materials, and by conducting them in an attractive well equipped learning environment. I can ensure excellence in my seminars by limiting participation to small groups, so that information can be covered effectively and I can address individual needs within a three to four hour time frame.

But there's one minor fly in the salad dressing. In order for me to generate a profit, the participants would have to pay more to attend the seminar, to cover the cost of extensive and expensive course materials, attractive surroundings and individual attention. So I can deliver excellence but efficiency, and economy suffer.

What I could do, of course, is charge less and deliver economy by expanding participation in the seminars, handing out less course material, and using less well equipped and attractive surroundings. More economy but less excellence. I could deliver efficiency by conducting the seminars by audio, video or satellite transmission. More efficiency and more economy but less excellence. You can't eat your cake and have your speedo too - nobody gets it all. But as Meatloaf says, "Don't be sad, 'cause two out of three ain't bad."

Recognize that in order to stay in business and generate an acceptable level of profit, compromise among the three E's is inevitable. The challenge for a business owner is to figure out which two of the three are most important to his or her target market, then find ways to consistently deliver those. Remember, even Superman had to compromise on some things, faster than a speeding bullet, able to leap tall buildings, but would you really want to wear that outfit?

In my experience, when it comes to making significant product or service purchases, such as homes, cars, vacations, accounting services, financial planning services, insurance services or even decorating services, buyers can be loosely grouped into three categories.

1. **Performance buyers.** One group buys on product or service performance. The primary value associated with the product or service, in their minds, is performance. Will the product or service do what it's supposed to do and is it likely to do it over a specified period of time? While there is a limit to what a performance-focused buyer will pay, price is not the primary issue in the buying decision.

2. **Personal service buyers.** Another group place great value on personalized service or advice. Again, price is a factor in their decision, but the primary value associated with the purchase is personal attention, unique services and results-generating advice.

3. **Price conscious buyers.** The third group are the bargain basement buyers. You may think everyone is a price conscious buyer. True, to a point. But think again. Take five minutes to consider what you have bought in the last 12 months, you'll probably recall making at least some purchases where price was not the primary or value factor in your buying decision. For some, price is the holy grail, and the words bargain and lowest price will always have them looking past performance or added service.

Every service provider eventually has to decide what category of customer they want to appeal to. You then need to focus your efforts on filling the needs and bringing value to the people in that category. We are living in an age of specialization and it is becoming more difficult and less profitable to try to be all things to all people. Remember why you went into your business and the customer profile you developed. Anytime you hear someone exclaim, "Geez, that's a lotta money - for what you do," flee from the scene as fast as your roller blades will carry you.

Doug

WAITER - A BOTTLE OF YOUR BEST

Dear Doug,

I hope I made some sense on the phone Thursday night. The universe is finally and truly unfolding as it should. I'm writing to you on a wonderful Sunday evening after a fantastic week-end. The reason for all this euphoria of course is because, as I told you on Thursday, my first major contract. I've got a contract to decorate the interiors of nine, yes, you read correctly, nine dining rooms in a hotel chain that is growing very big in the north-west U.S. and throughout western Canada. I've finally been given the chance I've been working so hard to get. This contract will make a huge difference to my business. It will ease the financial stress and create an opportunity for me to make an impact in my target market sector.

I feel like a solid foundation for my business is about to be poured, a foundation strong enough to support my plans for the future. I'm now really in business! Funny how a collection of five words brought together to form a simple sentence, can look to me like my personal declaration of independence. I sit here staring at them on my computer screen. I manipulate them so they fill the screen. I say them out loud, sing them to myself and shout them out for the walls to hear. Saying them just sounds sooo, goood. I'm just so incredibly happy.

I'm sure this letter isn't making any more sense than the phone conversation did, and I'm not sure whether right now I'm writing it for you or me.

Anyway getting back to my weekend, Friday night was the big celebration. You know the drill, round up the friends and let them stroke my ego. Share a few glasses of champagne and a glass or two or three of wine. Enjoy a whole night of self centered me'isms. End up solving the real issues and problems of the world and reflect on what a great life it is. It's so great to have friends who genuinely appreciated the significance of the celebration, who understood what it meant to me and who paid the bar tab.

Most of Saturday was spent in deep seclusion recovering from Friday. I did manage to pull myself together for a dinner with some friends on Saturday night, one of whom is a terrific guy named Rob. I've mentioned him a couple of times, he's the guy with the desk top publishing business. He and I have been sort of going out for a couple of months. He has been operating his business for almost ten years. His business model is very different from mine. He limits his clients almost exclusively to those who helped him in the early years and with whom he has a very close working relationship. He takes on only enough business to be able to provide personal service and does not out source any of the work he does. He is also a confirmed work from home advocate, and has no interest in working from a commercial office. He likes to remind me, he has been able to build a very profitable business, while enjoying a satisfying lifestyle. He and I have some very animated discussions about my wanting to build my business to the maximum potential that it has, and his desire to stay small.

Rob and I and two other couples went to a small local bistro for some very good seafood, and to continue as he said "a quieter saner celebration of my new found success." You know, I have come to realize there is a real upside and downside to having a commercial interior design business. The upside is, I get to do market research in some terrific bars and restaurants. The downside is, while I'm in them I spend too much time critiquing the layouts and color schemes, and not enough time enjoying the food; oh well, we all have our cross to bear. Strange isn't it, how a wonderful time in the present will trigger great memories from the past. During dinner I had a flashback to some of the great evenings we all used to share over dinners at Jonathan's. How is the dashing and debonair man himself? Tell him there are some places here that compare with the quality of food and service he offers, but none come close to the ambiance created by his impeccable style, grace and old world charm. That should be good for a glass of wine when I get back to visit.

What a fabulous few days this has been. I've got goose bumps just writing this. Strange, if I let myself, I could get weepy, but this time it would be the good weepies. I guess the lows and now the highs of these last months are catching up. I feel very introspective and quietly confident. The experience I've gained with my small clients will now be put to the test. I can't wait to get started.   I think I'd better try to wrap this up, settle down a little, stabilize my emotions and get some rest. The next few months I will be living a dream come true, and I will be a very, very, busy 'entrepreneur'.

Oh, almost forgot. I have joined together with five other small business owners to form what we are calling an entrepreneurs alliance. We are going to meet casually once a month to discuss various concerns and issues that confront each of us, or might be common to all of us. I think it will be fun and very educational.

Cheryl

FOCUS ON THE POSITIVES

Dear Cheryl,

Just a few general observations and comments in this letter, kind of a follow up to our phone conversation last week-end. Being the mega success you've suddenly become, I'm not sure you'll even have the time to look at it. If you don't, at least it'll make good kindling for when you're sitting in front of the fire, basking in the glow of your new found success.

Just think, no more nights lying awake with the 'will I make it' anxiety sweats, wondering if and when your efforts will pay off. No more wondering if you'll ever be able to put some of that black ink you've been saving down on your balance sheet. Instead, you can now toss and turn with the 'can I satisfy the customer' anxiety sweats. Worries about getting the order now replaced by worries about filling the order, doing the job to the customer's satisfaction, bringing it in on time and on budget, and then wondering where the next one will come from when this one is finished. You didn't want to get out of the habit of sleeping more than five hours a night anyway, right?

Running your own business has got to be the greatest love-hate relationship in the world. By the way, it's great that things in your personal life are coming together for you as well. It seems to me it was only a few months ago that I was doing the old psychological prop up. Now you're breaking out the champagne. Who said this business stuff was tough? Little more than a year in business and you've generated your first significant contract. I hope you've taken the time to make a copy of your first retainer cheque and framed it. By what you tell me your customer obviously did their homework before awarding you the contract, so feel good about yourself. You went after it, you did it right and you got it. Reward yourself, take a few minutes to bask in the glow of success. Then get it in gear, rev up your energy, and put yourself to the test. I love it when a plan comes together, don't you?

What a great idea to form an entrepreneurs alliance group. Your idea of getting together with others like you and discussing concerns and issues is a good one. I also think limiting your group to six participants will give everyone a good opportunity to be a contributor during your meetings. The people in the group sound, from the way you described them like they share some of your traits but are diverse enough to bring various points of view to the discussions. Let me know how your kick-off meeting goes. Yes, I'll be happy to send you some of my seminar topics and notes to help get some discussions going. Thanks for the honorary membership.

It sounds like you have a good mix of seasoned and rookie entrepreneurs in the group, so I thought the following might be of interest to everyone. You and your colleagues may want to remind each other that, although the operation of any business brings with it ongoing challenges to overcome, there is little to be gained during any brain storming session by dwelling exclusively on problems. Equal time should be given to thinking about and talking about the rewards that come with success, what everyone is striving to achieve and what they enjoy most about the challenge of their business. So much of the talk about small business entrepreneurship in the media seems to center on how difficult it is to survive and get through the first year or two. Statistically speaking that may be true, but I think it puts too much of a negative spin on the whole process of becoming an entrepreneur and building a business. Entrepreneurs, in practical and philosophical terms, are inherently positive-thinking optimists. All the talk about statistical failure may be true, but no successful entrepreneur ever thinks of him or herself as a statistic. Statistics are for losers. Spare us the statistics of failure. How many people try and how many fail doesn't interest us. We're interested in the success of one small business, ours. Everyone knows getting a profitable business launched isn't easy. But don't flog it to death. When you get together with your group, don't contribute by being a dooms - day disciple, instead remind everyone that sitting around thinking about how cold the water is going to be when the boat goes down, isn't going to help keep it afloat. You wouldn't be in business for yourself, if you didn't think the worst days working for yourself didn't beat the best days working for someone else.

The success of each of the businesses operated by the people in your group will be driven in large measure by their being able to; provide quality goods and services, delivered on time, at competitive prices. Consistently meeting those standards will lead to recognition and acceptance among your target customers. Maintaining those standards will lead ultimately to long-term customer loyalty.

You can do a quick and simple analysis of how successful your business is likely to be, by asking yourself the following questions:

Ask yourself if:

- Your product or service is designed to consistently meet or surpass the needs of your customers.
- You are prepared and able to make adjustments quickly to your product or service, to meet changing customer wants and needs.
- You have a system in place to consistently stay in touch with your customers to remind them of the availability of your product or service or of their previous satisfaction with your company.

Here's something everyone in the group can have some fun with. It's a formula for making changes or breaking habits. It might be a fun exercise for everyone. Have everyone take action to make a small change in something they aren't satisfied with, try the formula and report their results at a future meeting.

▸ *Plan a small change in something you're not satisfied with.*
▸ *Carry out the change over a 30-day cycle.*
▸ *Note the positive or negative consequences of the change.*
    ▸ *From the results decide whether to:*
    ▸ *Adopt the new*
    ▸ *Try another way*
    ▸ *Return to the old*

Doug

To escape being criticized, do nothing, say nothing, and be nothing.

A TOP TEN POSITIVES LIST

Dear Doug

The Entrepreneurs Alliance thanks you. We got our first meeting off the ground last Thursday evening. What a terrific experience. Everyone was friendly but somewhat reserved for the first half hour or so, but things began to pick up right around the pouring of the second glass of wine.

We followed your suggestion and decided, because it was our first meeting, to make it a 'positives first' meeting. It was really fascinating and inspiring to hear people who are just like me, talk about their ambitions and expectations. Every single one of us agreed that we had grown as people and increased our self confidence through the experience of setting up our businesses. It was also interesting to note that while four of us were intent on taking our businesses as far as they would grow, two of the group were just as intent on taking on only enough business to generate a comfortable income and run their businesses from home. A couple of the group surprised me by saying that if the right corporate job offer came along, they would be tempted to go back into the 'real job' world. Everyone had his or her ideas of what the positives were in running your own business, so we decided to make a top ten list. We had a lot of fun making up the list, and I thought you might enjoy seeing it.

1. You can make things happen.
2. You are the committee.
3. For better or worse, you're the boss.
4. Yes, no or maybe decisions are yours to make.
5. When you look in the mirror, the person responsible looks back.
6. The bottom line is, the bottom line is - yours.
7. You make the choice, what kind of business do you want your business to be.
8. You can make a business out of your lifestyle, or you can make a lifestyle out of your business.
9. You can get paid for doing what you like to do.
10. When you look around what you see is what you built.

We ended the meeting by having some fun with your personal change formula. We each made a declaration of what we intend to change over the next 30 days and we are going to review our results at the next meeting. I'm going to try to cut down on my caffeine intake. Just another small step toward the new more moderate me.

Cheryl

YOU CAN'T JUST SWING A BIG CLUB

Dear Cheryl,

I'm glad to see you and your friends are having some fun with your entrepreneurs alliance. The list is great, I enjoyed seeing it, nice to see they share your off beat sense of humor. It was very kind of you, but not really necessary to send me pictures of you and your friends on the golf course at this time of year. Incidentally, it is common knowledge that no self-respecting entrepreneur should be on the golf course for at least the first three years of being in business. Has your nose become a little chafed by the grindstone already? I'm also aware, you know all too well that we still have six weeks of winter, followed by thirty days of the great spring melt, to go through, before it will be dry enough to play here. You wouldn't be trying to rub it in a bit, would you? I notice you made lots of mention of the flora and fauna on the course you were playing. Does that mean you had plenty of opportunity to study it while trying to find your ball? And how convenient that you didn't mention your score! I'm planning a little golf excursion of my own to Bermuda in two weeks, I will send you some pics of a real golfer in action.

I have been waiting for the right time to add a few thoughts on the importance of a strong and healthy self-concept to those I talked about in one of my early letters. I have been thinking a lot about what I wrote to you in that letter. A healthy self concept is so important to an entrepreneur, I wanted to make sure I had covered all the bases. I believe your self concept is what fuels your positive energy. Building any business means coming face to face with physical, emotional and psychological stresses and strains, particularly in the early years. You need high reserves of positive energy to manage and work through those stresses and strains.

What comes first the chicken or the egg, the cart or the horse, the hole or the donut? All fascinating questions to be sure. One question I think will have more impact on your life as an entrepreneur is this. Will you feel good about yourself more often because of what you accomplish, or will you accomplish more because of how good you feel about yourself? I think one thing we can both agree on is, nowadays, you have to perform at a higher than average level just to be average.

Your level of performance is a direct reflection of your self concept. When you feel good about yourself on the inside, you create reserves of positive energy that enable you to sustain a higher level of performance for longer periods of time. You have the chance to raise the bar on your personal performance when your self concept is healthy and well fed. Your self concept will even help you deal with the daily doses of stress that are a part of every entrepreneur's diet.

For the most part, four factors will determine how successful you will be.

1. The knowledge you have
2. The skills you possess
3. The attitude you maintain.
4. How well you are able to blend all three together

Having a healthy self concept won't take the place of knowledge or skills or the right attitude, but it can give you the stamina, drive and determination that's needed to put them all together in a winning package.

A strong, self concept will increase your reserves of positive energy. Enabling you to work through longer days at higher levels of efficiency. You find yourself better able to cope with daily ups and downs, with less moaning and groaning and you won't find yourself getting bogged down as often in the 'poor me' syndrome.

Here's a little story about the importance of being able to call on reserves of positive energy when you need them. You know I wouldn't make something like this up! It is a true, but little known fact, that positive energy has played a role in the evolution of people since the time of the cave entrepreneur. For the cave entrepreneur, positive energy was a factor in daily survival. Positive energy evolved as a means of dealing with life's daily little aggravations, like finding yourself a meal without becoming a meal yourself. Most of the problems the cave entrepreneur faced could be overcome by either swinging a very large club at them, or running very quickly away from them. In each case a rush of positive energy was required. It was needed to furnish the strength to lift and swing the big club, or to energize the leg muscles in order to flee quickly from the scene. So, in fact, it is a little know fact that it was positive energy that gave the cave entrepreneur time to invent the wheel, tame fire, and become fashion-conscious. A healthy self-concept can help you swing a big club at your problems today too.

Doug

IT WON'T ALWAYS BE
THIS TOUGH WILL IT?

Dear Doug,

Tell me that the first year or two in business are the toughest. Eighteen months and counting and I don't want to have ten or twenty more like this to look forward to. Even if you have to lie, go ahead and do it. There is a time for the truth and a time for a little creative lying, feel free to be creative. Don't misunderstand me I'm not really whining. I think I'm just looking for some compassion. I feel very sorry for the next person who looks at me and says "boy are you ever lucky not to have to go to work everyday," or "I'm thinking of starting a business - I think it would be a lot of fun."

I realize I had a better start-up year than lots of people and things are continuing to go well and for that I'm truly thankful. I guess part of working on your own is realizing that if you want a pat on the back you're going to have to reach around and do it yourself. I've got to think that for a lot of people who work on their own the lack of positive reinforcement and peer recognition can be frustrating and at times even depressing. If there is one aspect of working on my own I really didn't expect would have the impact that it has had and that I wasn't prepared to deal with, it is the isolation factor.

I think most business people, especially if you're on the front line dealing with the public are pretty gregarious, and sociable. I was sitting alone one morning last week, having a coffee break when my mind wandered back to the old days and the old gang at work. If you stop to think, a lot of people spend at least as much time during a work week conversing with and interacting with their work colleagues as they do with friends and family. When access to workplace interaction, the grapevine and the daily banter of workplace friends and colleagues is cut off and that door is closed, the feeling can become almost claustrophobic.

I think one of the most valuable lessons I've learned over these last eighteen months is to make the effort to get out and connect with other small business people like myself. You have to make an effort to reach out and build new workplace friendships with other entrepreneurs based on the commonality of your situations, just as people in large companies do.

I find that I now have a network of colleagues that I keep in touch with at least weekly and sometimes daily by gathering around the techno - water - coolers, we know as email, phone and fax. Participating in the meetings of my entrepreneurs alliance group is turning out to be a valuable source of fun, ideas, information, as well as being an energy booster and stress reliever. Attending the monthly meetings of the networking group, keeps me tuned in to a bigger small business picture and helps me stay in touch with potential customer referrals, and I find it just a great way to kick-off a day.

I'm looking at taking two big steps in the next few months. No, not that. Rob and I are in a dating relationship, but that's it for now, I think. I'm going to move into a commercial office building and hire three maybe four people to help with the workload. I've put some new numbers together based on the current business in house and projected revenue for the next twelve months and they support the added cost of the office and personnel. I'm incredibly busy with the clients I have, particularly with the hotel chain. I find myself really short of the time I need to prospect for new business, and I know the future cash flow danger in that. I have decided to look for some administration, sales and design help. I'm sending you the latest numbers and projections, so let me know what you think. I'm starting to feel and sound like a real walking talking business person. Pretty soon I'll be having my people, call your people.

Cheryl

When in doubt,
mumble.
When in trouble,
delegate.
When in charge,
ponder!

LESSONS FROM REAL LIFE

Dear Cheryl,

You are so right, as you mentioned on the phone last week, the time is not just flying by, it's rocketing past. Your company is beginning to show improved revenue and profit, exciting, isn't it? Nice, steady, manageable growth...a pretty solid accomplishment, all in all. With your reputation growing and your business connections increasing, it looks like you're well-positioned to continue moving forward in the years ahead. It's great that you're feeling both more confident and more relaxed, you should be. You've been through what I would call the entrepreneurs' initiation, and now you are ready to move forward as a small business professional. I know you've thought long and hard about taking the next step, and you're right, it is a huge one. Moving out of the old home office and into a commercial building is exciting and a little scary. But considering the growth in your revenue, and looking at your projections for next year, your decision to expand outside your home and hire the first members for your team, is a good one.

In one of your recent letters, you noted "how quickly the theories get lost in the everyday realities." I couldn't agree with you more. I still believe it is important to have a fundamental understanding of the theories behind good business practices, but you're right, real life experiences are our greatest source of education. I have been working on an article for my newsletter which I've titled Applying Real Life

Lessons. I will let you have a sneak peak at it as I think it follows very closely the thoughts you mentioned in your letter. It compares some of the myths about entrepreneurship with the daily reality of operating a successful small business.

The first real life lesson I think most of us learn very quickly is that while business plans are vital to success, they should not be chiseled in stone. The next lesson is that while a good business plan reflects the size of the business you intend to operate, there is too much paper wasted on overly detailed business plans for the average small business. Try thinking of it in these terms. The bigger the business, the more trees that need to be cut to produce the business plan. Most small business start-ups need a business plan painted with broad brush strokes, while still having enough meat and potato details to satisfy the criteria of lenders and any potential investors you may be trying to attract. My experience has been that most business plans in the small business sector contain too much detail and try to cover too much ground. It's great to have an idea of what you are going to do and how you intend to do it, but don't get into paralysis by analysis. There is no real logic in thinking that you are going to be able to figure out every eventuality that may occur in the future of your business. My experience has been that much of what you thought was going to happen, won't and a lot of what you thought wouldn't, will. The key to a good business plan is to look at it like a flight plan. You need to know your starting point and your destination, and you need to set a course that will get you there, but you must have enough flexibility in the plan to deviate from your course to get around any rough weather you encounter along the way. My final thought on the business plan is this: keep it handy. Do something that most people don't - actually refer to it once in a while. After all, if you wrote it, it should be pretty interesting reading.

There is one myth that has grown to urban legend status which has little to do with how creative ideas come to be real life. New, innovative, workable ideas don't just spring fully developed into entrepreneurs minds as they sit watching re-runs of Seinfeld.

This flash-of-brilliance, birth-of-the-next-great-Microsoft theory is certainly a nice one, but it is more fantasy than real-life reality. When you look closely, most businesses are the end product of a number of related components coming together.

The idea, and the entrepreneur and the skill set needed to make it happen, begin to come together often because of a change in circumstances or a new need in the life of the entrepreneur. Whatever the reason, a business idea usually emerges when an entrepreneur combines his or her experiences, after mastering the fundamentals of the yet-to-be-discovered business on someone else's time.

I think entrepreneurs have to constantly remind themselves to live the day-to-day reality of their business, but at the same time, not stop dreaming the dream. When you begin your business, you may find yourself staring eyeball-to-eyeball, on an almost daily basis, with the twins of discouragement: problems and adversity. You do have to face the facts and deal rationally with the issues of the day. But in terms of how you think and what you dream, you must continue, from day one, to visualize in the positive. You cannot ever afford to ignore reality and you can't spend the time you need for implementing constructive activity in some kind of mind warp, wishing your problems away. But you do need to be able to see through the daily problems to the opportunities that lie ahead. And you need to be able to visualize those opportunities in a way that makes it possible for you to paint your vision of a better tomorrow in practical, realistic and easily-understood terms for everyone involved in your business.

A lesson that most entrepreneurs learn almost right out of the starting blocks, is that recovery is 90 percent of the game. How you recover from your mistakes (and you will have your fair share), is more important than spending all your time trying to avoid them. Mistakes are a by-product of growth. Rational analysis of how to correct every mistake doesn't always give you the right answer to the problem. Be willing to experiment with your solutions.

Another lesson that, for most people takes a little longer to learn, is that the world is a pretty big pie. Yes, you need to be ready to compete, but in every business sector there is room for more than one winner. Any good new business idea, or improvement to an existing one, will always draw competition. In some cases, your competitors may be better financed or have other superior resources to yours. Accept the fact that you will face stiff competition. Don't focus all your energy on trying to figure out what your competition is doing, because you may lose track of what your customers want *you* to do. Instead, work toward executing your idea better than anyone else. Work on refining your business, and always be on the look out for value-added opportunities to bring to your customers. Never underestimate or overestimate your competitors. Have respect for them, but don't drive yourself crazy worrying about what they are going to do next. Be proactive, not reactive, in your business. And when a competitor comes up with a better idea or way of doing things, don't hesitate to adopt their strategy, replicate it and make it your own.

Some lessons need to be learned from the experience of others, because you can't afford the time or the expense of learning them yourself. A lot of grief, time and money can be saved by taking some of your marketing cues from those who have gone before.

One marketing lesson that you can be sure will make a difference to the success of your business is to take decisive initial action. Be bold in your approach to marketing your business. If you are a late comer to the party, you can't expect anyone to notice you unless you make the right entrance. If you are going up against established competitors, you need to do something different to draw attention. You can't quietly creep into the hearts and minds of your potential customers, you must do something to get them to notice you.

When you do decide on a marketing initiative, make sure you measure the results of your efforts. If you don't, you'll be like the blind pig that occasionally finds an acorn. You can't afford just to stumble over the occasional customer, you've got to know what is working for you and what isn't. If standard marketing formulas aren't working for you, try something different, but make sure you always measure the results.

There's another lesson you don't necessarily have to live to learn: don't operate with tunnel vision. There is more than one right and effective way to serve your customers and operate your business. When your strategies are working, with every day bringing nothing but sunshine, the temptation is to fall into the old 'if it ain't broke, don't fix it' sense of security. It's easy to convince yourself that what got you here, will keep you here, and nothing needs to be changed. You are safe and secure behind the walls of your procedural fortress. But right about then, someone will lob a problem over the wall that can't be handled by doing things the way they've always been done. If all you see is the problem, and all your concentration is on problem solving, you could end up missing the fact that someone may have thrown an opportunity at you. Deal with today, look to tomorrow and forget yesterday.

Doug

On the whole, we all want to be good, but not too good, and not quite all the time!

BUILDING A
SERVICE COMMITMENT

Dear Cheryl,

I can understand with your mounting work load that you are going to have to do less writing and more calling over the next couple of months. That's not a problem I'll keep writing and you keep calling. You said recently that running your own business has made you more aware of and in some cases more critical of the way others operate theirs.

Isn't it interesting how when our circumstances change we notice things we had never paid much attention to before. The classic example of course is when you purchase a car. Almost immediately, you notice that hundreds of other people seem to have the exact same taste in color and style of car that you do. It isn't that everyone, having heard of your renowned and impeccable taste in cars, was waiting for you to make a decision so they could then run out and copy it. It's of course, because before you purchased your car, you weren't looking for and didn't have the same interest in one particular model and color of car.

I believe your observations concerning service, or rather the lack of it, results from looking much closer at it and having a keener interest in it. You are probably receiving the same level of service that you always have, in some cases outstanding, in others the classic service with a groan. You just haven't been as keyed into it until now.

Do you sometimes wonder if you are the only one buying and reading all those books being written on the service difference and how to profit from a service commitment? I have friends who are making a very good livings, thanks mainly to large companies who bring them in to do seminars on the benefits of customer service. For the participants, I think it must be like the old egg on the spoon races we used to have during picnics. When they leave the seminar, they have their eggs balanced nicely on their spoons, but by the time they get back to their jobs, the eggs have fallen off, the spoons aren't much good without the eggs and so they get discarded, and everyone and everything goes back to the way it was.

In a lot of companies, service is like the weather. Everyone talks about it but no one seems to be able to do anything about it. Do you see the obvious positive in all of this? Of course you do; As a small business entrepreneur, you want to make sure you're not talking about it, you want to make a commitment to doing something about it. Make the extra effort, spend a few extra dollars if you have to, invest some extra time if needed, but build on service.

You observed that businesses on the front lines of customer contact seem to be suffering the most service deficiencies. Of course, the degree of service varies according to the end use product or service. A smile and a simple, 'have a good day' is quite acceptable when spoken by someone wearing a cardboard hat. A smile and a, "try looking in aisle four" is probably all that can be expected from someone working in any company whose name ends in Depot. But in a small businesses which markets high end products or services like yours, the service offered has to be in sync, and match the rhythm and tempo of the customer's expectations. Your customers must constantly be satisfied and occasionally pleasantly surprised, by the level of service you bring to your relationship with them. Bear in mind, as you begin to hire employees, that good service has everything to do with staff training, motivation and compensation.

I suppose I might accept the trade-off of lower service for lower prices, but I never seem to notice any long-term or significant drop in the prices offered in places that are self serve, do you? Self serve, what a great marketing euphemism for no serve! Have we become a population of second-rate customers? Why else would we put up with this?

While we like to shake our heads and feel somehow superior when we see line-ups of people patiently and humbly waiting for goods and services in other parts of the world, we just have to look around in a bank to see the same thing happening to us. The box store phenomenon, with its culture of low prices, no service and no product knowledge continues to grow, so maybe as is so often the case, we get exactly what we deserve.

It has been my everyday experience that the small business service sector is the only one, on the whole, that offers customers the kind of idealized service we so often read about. In fact, the lack of follow through the big guys make on their commitment to service, makes it that much easier for small business entrepreneurs like you, who are willing to put the extra effort into their service to capture more customers and develop long-term, mutually beneficial and profitable relationships with them. Service is the game, customer loyalty is the pay-off and the door is wide open. We are in the throes of unparalleled growth in small business enterprise across North America.

In business today, it seems as if the wheel turns within the wheel. Big business counts on small business, not just as a supplier of goods and services to the mother ship, but increasingly, to fill customer service requirements. There is much irony in this because this very trend to outsourcing has been one of the factors in a lot of big company downsizing.

Pass on your commitment to quality service to your team. Help them understand the upside potential that can be generated from satisfied customers, and the downside damage that can result from poor service. In your specialty service sector, you will find yourself dealing with customers who will be very conscious of the trade-off between the price they pay and the service they get.

Doug

OUTGROWING
THE HOME OFFICE

Dear Doug

I sat bolt upright in bed at about 4:00 am this morning. No, it wasn't the left over pizza. It suddenly became painfully obvious to me that another of my many business deficiencies was about to be uncovered. I've never been in a position to advertise for and hire anyone before. I've never really conducted an applicant interview. All of that was looked after by human resources in my previous life. What if I make the wrong decision? I can't afford to go through a process of hire, tryout and fire. I need to get it right the first time. These are the people who will be at my side literally and figuratively for the foreseeable future. The office space I have rented, provides for only one semi private office and an open work area for administration, sales and design. It is going to be crucial that I get along with each of them and they get along with each other.

The ad is ready to go into the paper this week. I'm asking for written resumes and I expect to be interviewing the candidates by the end of next week. I don't want to end up using my 'gut instinct' when hiring these people. Any suggestions to improve my chances of making the right decision the first time. I need to put a qualified, enthusiastic and creative team together. It's beginning to look like another climb up the learning curve, for yours truly.

In spite of my trepidation about the hiring process, I am really excited about leaving my home office and setting up in the new location. I finally got the office with the window. The building is about 10 years old with a mix of small business tenants. It is about a thirty minute drive from where I live. I'll send some photos when everything is in place and operable. Do you recall my mentioning being referred to a health care organization a couple of months ago? Well it turns out, they operate ninety health services clinics in Washington, Oregon and California. They were looking at renovating their existing clinics in order to standardize the layout and make them more patient friendly. I was asked to submit some design and decorating ideas for improving the patient waiting areas. They have chosen me to work on the 14 clinics they operate in and around Seattle as a pilot project and if all goes well, they will contract with me to do the remaining sixty-six clinics they operate. I attended a three day planning session at their offices in Newport Beach last week and we are in the process of finalizing and fine tuning the design and themes they have chosen. This will be my first contract outside of the food services industry and should create lots of additional opportunities. It will also mean I am definitely going to have to get into my new office facilities and get some people hired, as quickly as possible.

Cheryl

HIRING THE RIGHT PEOPLE

Dear Cheryl,

Let's see if some of these thoughts will help you in your hiring process as you recruit the first members of your team. You need to have all your communicating, listening, decision-making and good old fashioned people skills well-oiled and working in top form when you set out to do your hiring. Take it from an old camper, hiring the right people can be like adding the right wood to your fire. With the right wood, you get more heat and less smoke. Hiring the right people will accelerate the growth of your business. Hiring the wrong people will be like throwing green wood on your fire. You'll get very little heat and enough smoke to smother you and everything around you. Hiring the wrong people can choke the life out of your business and bring any progress you've made to a screeching halt. Nothing like adding a little more pressure to your life, is there? Oh well, it may help you burn a few calories, during your nightly tossing and turning marathon. (You're welcome.)

With the right people on your team, you can move your business forward with confidence. A quick reality check here, hiring the right people is never an exact science. However, you can and should avoid relying exclusively on the, 'I've got a good feeling about this person' method. Get some qualifying procedures into your hiring by starting with job descriptions. Develop a written job description that best describes the functions included in the job being offered. Then write out a skills check list and personality profile for the type of person you would think could do the job and who you would be comfortable working with. Be careful here, you aren't looking for clones, leave some room for personality diversity. Make sure the skills list is not too specific, you are going to need people who might be specialists but who are also flexible enough to pitch in and help in other areas when necessary.

Give equal weight to the personality profile and the skills check list when evaluating a candidate for the job. Make sure that anyone who applies for an opportunity with you, furnishes a complete written resume. When you conduct an interview, remember that the purpose of the interview is to help you find reasons to hire the person. You are looking for proof that the applicant has the qualities and abilities you're looking for. Prepare yourself to conduct the interview, by writing out open-ended how, who and what style of questions to use during the interview. Include specific questions about situations candidates would likely encounter on the job. Listen attentively to the answers and do not interrupt, make notes. You will learn more with your eyes and ears open and your mouth shut.

About the closest to perfection most people will ever come is when they are filling out a job application!

In addition to learning about job qualifications, you are also conducting the interview to find out if the candidate possesses the type of personality and character traits you will be comfortable with. One way to get a handle on this is to pick a general topic outside of the immediate business to discuss and see if any rapport develops. But avoid the temptation to ramble and keep the interview on target.

That's it for now. Once you get your team in place, you won't be making all the decisions all the time anymore. Keep in mind that there are four ways a decision can be reached. You can decide, you and someone else can decide, you can appoint someone to decide, or everyone can decide. Don't worry though, you still get to decide how the decision will be made.

Doug

DOING BUSINESS
WITH PEOPLE WHO PAY

Dear Cheryl,

A short note with some thoughts that might cause a stir at your next entrepreneurs alliance meeting. One key mistake I see many small business entrepreneurs making, is that too many times they put their focus and efforts into trying to do business primarily with the small and micro business sectors. You are not likely to fall into that trap because the target market for your services are primarily mid-sized to large companies. But for many small business entrepreneurs, doing business with people on the same level of the food chain doesn't work. The main problem is lack of money on both sides of the equation. All too often, small business people are strapped for operating funds and they begin to trade and barter their expertise and products among each other to replace the unavailable cash.

This may be fine for micro business hobbyists, and in small doses, for small business, but ultimately cash flow must be addressed. I always urge small business people to think in terms of doing business with the 20 percent of the people who issue 80 percent of the cheques, and that is mid-sized to large companies. Some small business owners tell me they don't go after big business accounts because either, they offer specialty products and services and can't seem to get through the maze to find the people with the decision-making power, or they are intimidated when making sales presentations because they don't have a background in sales. They need to increase their knowledge and improve their skills in the areas of personal selling and communicating. In other words, if they can't sit down with a customer, find out what the customer needs, and explain how they can help, without seeing the customer's eyes glaze over, they need help with their sales skills. It's never about selling what you have, it's always about providing what the customer needs, and most of those needs center on how to increase revenue, save time, improve performance or solve a problem.

Doug

Celebrate the profit!

GENERATING MORE REFERRALS

Dear Cheryl,

By the way you described your employees to me last week when you called, you've done a fine job of candidate assessment and hiring. Just think, you can now tell everyone, you have an administrative department (Beth and you), a sales team (Tom and you), and a design team (Karen and you). The people you've hired sound like they have the skills and characteristics to form the nucleus of a terrific team.

As for motivating them, I don't think you need to be overly concerned at this point. All the new excitement will carry the day for a while and your enthusiasm has always been highly contagious.

I was very pleased that you mentioned, the number of customer referrals is continuing to increase. The best measure of customer satisfaction are the two R's, repeat and referral. Continuing to keep your customer base satisfied, and just as importantly, reminding them of their satisfaction, will pay off in a steady and growing list of referrals. The quality of job you do for your current customers provides solid referral business from them now and repeat business from them in the future.

I think we all fall short of the mark when it comes to getting all the referral business we would like. Most of us, myself included, get too busy with the everyday business of running the business to always remember the importance of asking for referrals. Sometimes we think because we go out of our way to provide exceptional service, that will be enough. But, surprise surprise, it isn't. This may sound like a contradiction in terms, and kind of odd, but most referrals are not in fact, the result of providing great service. They are the result of consistently reminding your customers of the great service you have provided to them, and can provide for people they know.

You must consistently remind your customers of three simple things: this is what I do, this is how I do it and these are the results you can expect. Next, get in the habit of asking two simple questions: do you know of anyone who could benefit from the service I provide? Would you be willing to tell them about me? You have to decide for yourself how best to make this system work for you, but I would recommend some combination of personal contact, telephone contact and direct mail contact to make it most effective.

As you know, advertisers always emphasize that in order to have impact and create top of mind awareness, a product name must be in front of people on a consistent basis. The same principle applies to a successful referral generating system. I know you are very creative when it comes to mail-outs, so this should be easy for you. Send various reminders, to your customers regularly. I've used brochures, personal profiles, profiles on new staff members, reminders of the services we provide, testimonials from satisfied customers and simple one-page newsletters. Occasionally I enclose a personal hand-written note highlighting the importance I place on building my business through personal referrals. Give it a shot. It doesn't take as much time as you might think and the results certainly justify the time and effort.

I also believe people respond enthusiastically to a surprise reward of any kind. You might consider rewarding people who go out of their way to generate a referral for you. These tokens of appreciation don't have to be expensive. In this case, it really is the thought that counts. Your referral business is a great barometer of the satisfaction and loyalty of your customers. Keep a close eye on any drop in your number of referrals, as that can be an early warning sign of customer dissatisfaction.

Doug

QUALITY COMES FIRST

Dear Cheryl,

In response to the comments contained in your recent email, let me say that I agree with what you said about quality in business being hard to define. Here's my definition of business quality: quality is the result of a commitment to set your personal standards high enough to exceed customer expectations. I also believe that the quality image or reputation of any business begins with, ends with and is a direct reflection of the quality of the people working in it. As far as creating quality impressions with customers, I agree with your comment that it will be the people dealing directly with them who can make or break quality impressions. They are the ones who will be most visible and who must carry the quality flag for you. Because you are offering an expensive service in a niche market sector, you need to help everyone on your team, from your receptionist on up, understand the importance of leaving clients with a quality impression. They should strive to leave every client with a good impression of who they are, what your company does, and how everyone does it.

Positive attitudes and actions help your customers 'feel' the quality impression everyone should be trying to make. It increases their comfort level while doing business with you and it encourages them to feel confident in becoming a loyal customer activist. Loyal customer activists are the kind of people who want everyone to know how good you and your team are, they are a step above satisfied customers. They brag to their friends and business colleagues about the advantages of doing business with you. They become over time your most proficient, vocal and effective sales force.

Long-term, sustainable revenues and profits are generated by building a loyal customer following. Naturally everyone is always trying to make satisfied customers of everyone who deals with you, but it's the core group of loyal followers you develop, who will make operating your business more fun and more profitable.

The market you've targeted is small so the people in it are bound to compare notes on what they are getting from service providers like you. The upside and downside of doing business in a small market sector are one in the same, it's easier and quicker to make an impression and gain a reputation. The reputation you build will always reflect your attitude. Every business has an attitude and it's the people in the business that create it. When your customers are after-sale-sold by the quality service they received, your customer retention level will always be high and your referral business will always increase.

Cheryl, I know I'm talking to the already-converted when I talk to you about quality, but did you know research shows, satisfied customers will tell, on average, eight other people about their satisfaction and good experience dealing with you? What a great way to build your business! But dissatisfied customers will tell, on average, 20 other people about their misfortune in dealing with you. What a dismal way to destroy your business. Service and results are linked directly together. When results are less than expected, look both to the quality of service being offered, and the person offering it.

A short aside here. Don't forget the importance of building some quality into your life along with building it into your business. Don't be tempted to buy into the 12 hour-a-day, seven day-a-week model as the only one you can use to build your business. Have some fun, because if you can't do it in 10-hour days, five days a week, you aren't doing it right. Remember, one of the reasons you went into this was to build toward a prosperous retirement one day, not work yourself into an early and permanent one.

Doug

ATTITUDE DOES
MAKE A DIFFERENCE

Dear Doug,

I'm glad you got a kick out of the fax I sent you last week. I was really surprised when the reporter called me and said they wanted to do a story about me in the newspaper. The paper runs a feature story on a local entrepreneur every other week. Before you have to ask, yes I am enjoying my fifteen minutes of fame. We knew I could do it, right? Incidentally, as my fame grows, I will remember to occasionally mention your role as mentor to the stars. I am enjoying one of those great times in my life when the blue in my sky goes on forever. Last week in the middle of another frantic business triathlon; running through the mine fields, cycling across the high wire and swimming with the sharks, I found myself smiling and laughing to myself about how much just plain unadulterated fun I was having. I wasn't working at all, I was playing on my field of dreams, and I was loving it.

I dug out one of your tapes on attitude last week, stuck it in the tape player in my car and listened to it while I drove to work. Boy, I must be in a good mood these days!

I agree with your message that good things grow in a good environment and that our personal environment is controlled by our attitude. You also said, and I know this to be true, that "attitude impacts on everything we think about, try to do, and ultimately get done." I enjoyed the part when you mention why it's critical to our success that we take charge and ownership of the attitude that we build for ourselves. You're right no one is born with an attitude. It's something that's shaped by people, events and actions throughout our lives.

I had a great time listening to the Lego blocks analogy again. How building and maintaining a positive attitude isn't easy, but it can be fun. How we start our lives with an attitude lego set, and how different thoughts and actions influence how we put it together and what we build with it. I love the image of the Lego blocks being divided into positive and negative pieces. You point out that just like in real life, the negative pieces in the set outnumber the positives. I think how true, every time I hear you say that as people, places and things begin to have a negative impact on our attitude, we have to search frantically through the blocks to find new positive ones to rebuild with. You're so right when you say finding positive blocks may not sound like much of a challenge, until we realize that, throughout our lives, a lot of people want to throw out our positive blocks and help us build with the extra negative ones they have. I think what you mean is, we all have a choice in the blocks we choose to seek out and use in building our attitude, and we shouldn't let negative builders work on the project. You really struck a cord with me when you summed it up with the part about the

Nobody plays with my lego anymore!

cynics. You know, a cynics advice is always free and the value is reflected in the price.

I like the way you throw the responsibility for building our attitudes back in our laps. You hit the mark when you say, letting our attitude be build by people, places or things around us, is giving up on ourselves and giving in to circumstances. I found myself really thinking about how you say, it's never too late to change whatever circumstances we find ourselves in and circumstances are never permanent until we accept them. Anyway, I hope you enjoyed the ride to work with me as much as I enjoyed having you along. I'll call you on the week-end and catch you up on more of the good things that are happening.

Cheryl

GOING FROM
PLANNING TO ACTION

Dear Cheryl,

I'm still laughing at our conversation from last weekend. I'm greatly relieved to find that your sense of humor is still intact and as warped as ever. I was astounded when you mentioned you've gone past the two year mark since starting the business, where has the time gone. I loved comparing people stories with you. I guess by now you are realizing, as I said back somewhere in the past, that any business is first and foremost, a people business. The dynamics of dealing day-in and day-out with people in all their various guises, can lead to some interesting situations. I also agreed with your observations regarding the importance of business planning. Planning is one of the components of small business often relegated to the back burner once the business begins to operate. Oh sure, you have your original business plan, including your operating and marketing plans, but too often they are thrown into a desk drawer when the real stuff starts to hit the fan.

You need to make an effort to treat planning as an ongoing part of your business. Take it out of the drawer, and bring it into the light once in a while. Keep it in good shape by massaging it occasionally. It's important to remember you didn't carve your plan in stone. Think of it more like a Gumby that you bend and twist to fit the circumstances. Given that we are both dyed-in-the-wool free enterprisers and profit is a word we have great respect for, I think it should be easy to sell you on the concept of continuous action planning. In any business course worth it's entry fee, you are told all business operates in order to generate profit. The first step on the road to profit is to develop a business plan. The business plan then needs to be divided into short term easy to implement actions plans, with time lines.

When putting together a business plan you are usually working with someone else's planning model. You end up with too much big-picture planning and not enough everyday operational action plans, specific to your set of circumstances. The big picture business plan is the act of thinking out and writing down a plan and a budget which will give you the framework you need to get your business from where it is, to where you want it to be. Certain assumptions are built into the planning process such as assuming you know where to find a market for your goods or services and you will be able to provide them at competitive prices. It's the next stage where action planning comes in. You have to document the actions and time lines associated with getting your goods or services into the market you've identified. You need to figure out what actions and time lines are needed to produce the goods or services at competitive prices.

You can't develop action plans that work if you keep yourself hermetically sealed inside your business plan and focus only on it. You need to be sucking up as much information on shifting market conditions, consumer trends and competitor activity, as possible and using the information to develop easy to implement action plans.

The immediacy of the information is what is most important. Sure, it's good to read the futurists, who might tell you what the 10- or 20-year trends are, but leave most of that information for the high foreheads in big business to deal with. Your business is light on its feet and able to dance to a different drummer very quickly, so use that to your advantage.

Action planning should concentrate on three main target areas of your business. Look at ways you can, in the near term:

1. Increase sales
2. Improve efficiencies
3. Cut expenses

Right about now, I can almost see you putting down this letter and reaching for the phone to give me the old, 'where do you think I'm going to find time to do this' rant. In anticipation of your bleating and moaning, here's a process you can follow to develop an action plan which will make your business plan more relevant and effective.

- Take a week-end, away from the business and preferably, away from home.
- Take with you a rough written outline of the action plans you intend to implement.
- Review your most recent business year, comparing the results against the goals and objectives that you had set.
- Write down actions that are short term, reasonable and workable and will have an impact on your three target areas. Note: Avoid dreaming, the goal of this exercise is to develop workable, doable actions you can put to use right away.
- Re-read, re-think and re-write your goals and objectives for the coming year.
- When you feel satisfied with your actions plans, do the radical thing. Use them and use them right away.

That's it for now. Remember, planning to do something isn't the same as having a plan to get things done.

Doug

PUTTING AN
ACTION PLAN TO WORK

Dear Doug,

I'll be expecting a call the minute you get this letter. You have no idea how much I wanted to call with this news, but I thought you would get a kick out of seeing this note first. That was great advice in your recent letter about action planning. I took it to heart and decided to put your action planning formula to work. Rob and I took a rest and recreation weekend. We drove up to Vancouver and then took the ferry over to Vancouver Island. We then drove to a wonderful little out of the way Inn a few miles outside of a place called Naniamo.

The week before, I had reviewed this years results to date and compared them against what my goals and objectives were for the year. I then put together a rough outline of the action plan I intended to work on while I was there. I took some time on Saturday morning after breakfast, while Rob was taking a tennis lesson, to finalize my thoughts and develop a new action plan. I was pretty satisfied that it was reasonable and workable, but I wanted to review it with Rob and get his input before going ahead. We both discussed the plan casually while we walked through the grounds of the Inn on what turned out to be a glorious sunny and warm spring day. Later that afternoon, we re-read and re-thought the plan, made a few adjustments here and there, focusing on the parts of the plan we could implement right away.

When we finished, we decided as you suggested in your guidelines to do the radical thing and put the plan into action. So, here is the key component of the plan.

We are getting married!! How's that for action planning? We have set June 16th as the date. I know it's less than two months away, but you said to take action and we are. You'd better be here. Yes, that is a direct order. Don't you love the new assertive me?

We are going to have a small wedding of about 30 family and close friends. Rob's parents and a couple of his friends are coming all the way from Australia to attend. My Mother is crazed with excitement and is coming out 10 days before the wedding to help me with everything. God, save me!

I have a very personal favor to ask of you. I was hoping that since my Dad won't be with us that you would consider filling in for him. I really want you to be a part of my day, and I hope you can work your schedule to be here. We can nail down all the details when you call me. Oh, by the way, you can put me down as a believer in your action planning formula.

Cheryl

MANAGING YOUR
GROWING BUSINESS

Dear Cheryl,

I've got to hand it to you when you make up a plan of action, it's a beauty. You and Rob sounded totally wired when I called you. A lot of people have used my action planning format and had good results with it, but as usual, you've taken it one step further. It's certainly an honor to be asked to participate in your wedding. I've already worked my schedule around the date, and I'm looking forward to the wedding with great anticipation. I'm looking forward to meeting Rob, your new friends and the family you've told me about over the years. Don't worry, my lips are sealed, your deep dark secrets are safe with me. The couple of times I've talked to Rob on the phone, left me with a great impression of him, I know I'll enjoy sipping a couple of cool ones with him. See you in about eight weeks.

You said in one of your recent letters, that once you open your own business, the days get longer but the time gets shorter. I'm going to offer you some thoughts on how you might get more out of your time and shorten your day. You also mentioned hiring additional people for your team and I thought I'd offer some comments and tips on managing a growing business. I'm going to cover the subject matter in this and a future letter.

I have always been fascinated by time management, although I've never been much good at it. Mind you, that won't stop me from sharing the few ideas which have made a difference for me. For more in-depth advice, I suggest you consult someone who might be just a wee bit more organized than yours truly. But for what it's worth, here are the time-management principles that have worked for me.

Divide your tasks into high and low payoff activities, then build your day accordingly. Decide what your most productive time of day is and try to schedule high payoff activities for that period. Your most productive time is when you are usually at your physical, mental and emotional high point. For some people, it is early morning, for others midday and some people are night owls.

- Stay focused on the big picture.
- Don't get distracted easily and don't be putting out brush fires when the house is burning down.
- Set deadlines and timelines for major and minor projects and make whatever adjustments are needed to your schedule to meet those time objectives.
- Divide large projects into bite size pieces and don't always do things in a straight line.
- Yell loudly for help when you can put it to good use.
- Build a little reward or rest and mental health time into your project planning.
- For low payoff activities, set aside time to get done what you can, then move on. If you can delegate low payoff activities, do so, but make sure they are being done, so they don't sneak up on you later and bite you where it shows.

That's pretty much all I can offer you on time management. Now I'm going to offer you some thoughts on how to hire the right people to fill out your team as you continue to grow. I am going to have to break my thoughts into two letters. I'm really pushed for time (oops, bad management) so I will close out my thoughts in a letter in about a week.

The first thing you might want to do is to take some time out and make notes to yourself about why you decided to start your business.

Writing down your reasons may help you decide what characteristics the people you are going to hire are going to need, in order to be productive in the working environment you intend to manage. Yes, Cheryl, it's time to see if a manager's hat is going to fit on your entrepreneurial head. To help you get the thought process started, let me remind you of what I think are the right and wrong reasons for running a business.

Do you assume you can replicate your success by getting others to do things exactly the same way you did? Are you trying to clone your employees in your image? Do you think you can motivate your employees to do what you don't do and won't do? In my experience, any combination of these things leads to Troll management and business failure.

You know what Troll management is, don't you? It's when a manager spends most of his or her time hidden away in an office, door closed, blinds shut. Then once in a while they jump out yell and scream and scare everybody into working faster, with dire threats, then disappear again. A not overly productive style of management guaranteed to lead to disaster.

There are lots of good reasons for running your own business. I'll start with the one I think is most important. Wanting to bring knowledge, skills, positive attitude, and passion to a business you can call your own. You may also have some new, fresh ideas that you want to apply to already-proven ways of conducting business. Or you may have a burning drive and determination to succeed that can't be satisfied working for someone else. Maybe you believe that you will be doing something that in the short term will bring new satisfaction to you and in the long run will provide you with a satisfying and productive lifestyle.

Whatever your reason for starting a business, things are going to change as the business grows, and you will need to change with it. You will find it a huge change going from being responsible for everything, to being a manager, with the need to delegate. You can no longer be guided by 'me think', now it has to be 'we think'. What's 'mine is mine' must be replaced by 'what used to be mine is now ours'. That can be a tough transition for you to make.

Earlier I said that you must have an idea of the characteristics people will need in order to be productive working alongside you. There is one caveat to that, however. Remember that there is tremendous strength in bringing together diverse people and bonding them into a strong and determined team which can work in a demanding environment full of challenge and opportunity. When you've been on your own for some time, you get into a rhythm of dancing to the beat of your own drum. Don't expect everyone to pick up the same beat and do the same dance. When you are managing others, you may still be beating the drum but let them interpret the beat they hear and dance the way they're most comfortable. Your ultimate aim is to generate productivity and profitability, not put together a chorus line. Even before you begin your talent search, you might want to review some of these following thoughts. They may help the manager hat fit more comfortably.

Let prospective team members know that you intend to focus your concentration on the big picture. You will be concentrating on specific objectives and you expect team members to deal with solving small, everyday problems Make it clear they will be expected to manage and focus on their own areas of individual responsibility. Your job is to make sure the right firefighter is fighting the right size fire.

Let your team members know when they come to you with problems, they should also have a practical solution to offer. It's very important that you try to maintain your objectivity. It's always tempting to bring your subjective opinion into situations that have been mismanaged. Concentrate on improving the process, not affixing blame.

Bear in mind you are the leader and people will be looking to you to lead. When you are expected to make a decision, make it. Don't procrastinate. Make sure the course of action decided on is carried out quickly and correctly. Then forget it and move on.

Two of my favorite definitions of managing are these:
- Managing is the art of getting results through others.
- Managing is being able to recruit, train, maintain and manage a productive team, while attaining an acceptable level of profit.

Doug

DEFINING YOUR BUSINESS

Dear Cheryl,

Thanks for taking the time to call me with that referral. You are amazing, only a few weeks before the wedding and still you have the discipline to focus some of your time on business. No doubt this is the influence of my work ethic showing up.

It's kind of appropriate, you should bring up the idea right now that you think there might be a tendency for a lot of people running a small business to wander from their core business focus occasionally. It's certainly important to be able to define, in exact terms, what business we are actually in. It sounds a strange to have a business and not know what business you're in, but it happens, it goes on all the time and not just with small companies.

In fact, the computer sector is a great example. The sale of personal computers did not really take off until the people making them began to understand what business they were in. They eventually figured out they weren't in the hardware or software business, they were actually in the 'user friendly' business and that's when things began to happen.

I suggest, now, might be the right time for you to find out what business you are really in. Start by asking yourself and your customers a few very simple questions that might reveal some very surprising and worthwhile answers.

Ask yourself:

- What do I think motivates my customers to become my customers?
- What do I think motivates my customers to continue to be my customers?
- What do I think motivates my customers to bring other customers to me?
- What do I think my customers expect when doing business with me?

This can be a very illuminating exercise, so I suggest you do it at a time when you can relax and give it the attention it deserves. (A glass or two of your favorite wine might also be considered an integral part of the exercise.) Later, when you feel the time is right, survey some of your customers with the same questions, then compare their answers with yours. That should tell you what business you're really in. Enjoy the exercise and the wine.

Doug

HERE WE GROW AGAIN

Dear Doug,

Thank you for helping make the wedding everything I'd hoped it would be. What an incredible week leading up to it. I've never been so pampered, pushed, prodded and run off my feet. Everyone was so good about putting up with me. A wedding is one of those defining moments when you realize how important to you, your family and friends really are. You've got to admit, we know how to throw a wedding. Rob's family and his buddies certainly helped turn things into a week long festival. I'm so glad you and Rob were able to get out and get to know each other better in the week you were here. I'm sure playing some golf helped keep his mind off what he was getting himself into. I sure had my moments during the week, and everyone was incredibly good about putting up with me. I can't figure out why I felt so much pressure, it was only my wedding, not starting a business.

It was great to get away for a week, on our honeymoon. I felt a little cheated only being able to get away for one week. It's times like this when both Rob and I operating our own businesses can be just a tad annoying and inconvenient. I know, somebody has to keep the wheels of commerce and industry turning. We intend to get away for a two-week holiday later in the fall though, when business isn't so hectic. I know, good luck!!, but we really are going to do it. We're settling nicely into everyday life together. My place will be fine for both of us for a year and then our plan is to buy something where Rob can set up a larger and more functional home office.

I'm beginning to look around for larger office space and I'm in the process of hiring additional staff. I shouldn't have to ask this after all of the advice you've given me over the years but could you give me some pointers on how to keep my staff motivated. I'm finding as we continue to grow, the task of molding a cohesive, stimulated and motivated team becomes more challenging. I'm finding as we take on more employees the dynamics of operating the business are changing, just as you said they would. I am, as you know, a strong advocate of delegating authority and responsibility wherever and whenever feasible. What I would like is some advice on how to keep everyone motivated without having to spend quite as much of my time focusing on it. It seems to me there are so many intangibles that go into creating a dedicated workforce, and I'm sure I've missed at least a few. What I don't want to do is fall into the motivational 'flavor of the month' trap.

Cheryl

MOTIVATING YOUR TEAM

Dear Cheryl,

There is nothing mysterious about motivating people. In fact, let me set you straight right here: motivation is like a central heating system. It responds to outside conditions, but is controlled from the inside. What you need to do is just make sure the environment you create is conducive to growth, and that you do not interfere by radically turning the heat way up or way down, but simply ensure a comfortable temperature is always maintained.

Getting your people to buy into your concept is not rocket science. They need to know what's going on, they need to hear it from you, they need to know what you expect from them and they need you to be consistent in how you deal with them. You know the value I place on continuous creative change, but that doesn't mean changing your methods every time you change your underwear. People always need to know three vital things: they need to know the condition of the ship, where it's headed, and how the voyage is going. In that kind of motivational climate, people can grow and contribute positively to the success of the entire company.

You are the keeper of the environment in which you and your people live your work lives. They are not mind readers, it's up to you to share your vision, values, goals and objectives with them, and it's up to you to help them find a way to share in them. One way to get them involved is to let them know they will be expected to make responsible decisions in their areas of expertise, and they will be expected to take responsibility for the results of their decisions.

Let your staff know you are interested in their work and you will take the time to review it with them on a consistent basis, then make sure you do. Give them candid feedback and use positive reinforcement whenever you can. But if a screw-up occurs, let them know they screwed up and work with them to develop a new strategy to avoid the same mistake in the future.

Avoid having people come to you only to help them solve problems. Encourage them to share new thoughts and new ideas, as well. Work with them to help them develop an 'anything is possible' attitude and encourage them to use that attitude to create new opportunities for your business. Instill enthusiasm in your people for what they do, and pride in how they do it, and you won't have to toss and turn thinking of ways to motivate them. Cheryl, you might think these thoughts apply to larger businesses with more employees, but I believe it's important to set the tone of your company early on. Is it going to be a place where people want to come to work, or have to go to work?

Job satisfaction is a large part of on-the-job self motivation. Everyone in your company must feel a sense of personal achievement in the job they are doing and each must feel they are making a meaningful contribution to your stated objectives. You should see to it that people's jobs are made challenging and that they have to use the best of their abilities to meet the standards of that job. And always recognize a job well done, job satisfaction needs the warmth of recognition to flourish. People need to be recognized for accomplishments and achievements. The recognition doesn't have to be expensive or even always serious in tone. Have some fun with it.

At least once a month, look for something you feel is deserving of recognition. A hand-written 'job well done' note left for the recipient to find on his or her desk can mean as much, or more than a costly gift.

Remember to give your people permission to make mistakes. And when you assign a task, give them the appropriate authority to get on with it and get it done. All of these factors and more go into creating satisfying job experiences and contribute to positive motivational chemistry between you and your team.

If you want a quick way to rate yourself as a positive motivational influence, try this one.

- Have you talked with each person and agreed on their main targets and responsibilities and the standards of performance you expect?
- Are you prepared to recognize the contribution of each person with occasional verbal and written endorsements?
- When out-of-the-ordinary successes occur, are you prepared to acknowledge and build on them without delay?
- In the event of setbacks, do you begin the review of what happened by focusing initially on what went right, then moving on to a review of what went wrong? Do you do it objectively and dispassionately? Do you finish with a plan of action to guard against the same problem happening in the future?
- Should you be delegating more or giving your people more responsibility?
- Do you encourage your people to take courses or training that will help them develop personally and professionally and do you help compensate them for the costs involved?
- Do you demonstrate the trust you feel in your people?
- Do you sit down with your staff on a regular basis and review their performances with them?
- Do you make sure that each individual's financial reward matches their contribution to the company?

Doug

BUSINESS SLOWDOWNS HAPPEN

Dear Doug

Is this a plot to drive me nuts. We just got settled into the new larger facilities, the new people we hired are just getting up to speed and we find ourselves with business slowing down. Prior to the move, we were sailing along with a comfortable backlog of business, new business was coming in on target and lots of proposals were in the hopper. I can see now that over the last sixty days slowly but steadily business has been softening. I blame myself for getting so tied up with the move that I wasn't paying attention to the warning signs. The monthly sales figures were down over the past two months, but I chalked it up initially to the time of year and a little slowing of the work pace because of the move. I've taken a closer look at our backlog and the number of proposals we are working on and both are down from last year at this time. We are on forecast but that's only because of higher than expected sales in the first half of the year. Suddenly I feel like my baby is growing up and getting into trouble.

This is really the first significant downturn I've encountered since I began the business and needless to say it has me worried. My biggest concern is that this is happening during an abundance of good economic signs. The overall economy is strong. There's growth in our target market sector. That can mean only one thing, our market share is not increasing in step with the market. Our piece of a bigger pie is at best remaining stagnant. I've had meetings with my three department managers and we've gone over everything from who is doing what, to how should we be doing it. I'm going to send you the current figures along with the latest projections for the next quarter. I would appreciate your input.

I can't help feeling that I should have been on top of this and seen the indicators sooner. Maybe I have become too separated from the daily goings on. The growth of the company has forced me to delegate more and more responsibility and focus my attention on the big picture and our major clients. My department managers are terrific and they stay close to the minutia of daily operations. Maybe I need to set up a more structured internal reporting system. We've run a pretty free wheeling operation, but maybe with the growth we've experienced we need to build in more structure, before the wheels fall off the cart. I'm not in a panic, but I would be less than candid if I didn't admit this situation has taken some of the wind out of my sails. It has made me realize what a fragile thing, a small business really is.

Cheryl

MANAGING THROUGH
A SLOWDOWN

Dear Cheryl,

So business has slowed for you in the last few months, good reason to be concerned, no reason to be overly concerned.. Nothing goes straight up forever. I would say your concern, something is fundamentally wrong with your administration, operations, sales or marketing to be a little premature. Dr. Doug, would describe the situation this way. Your business shows signs of suffering from a flu bug, not an illness that requires radical surgery. Like any good parent you're concerned about the health of your child, even if it's only running a slight fever you want to be alert to any further problems, that's understandable.

Everything we reviewed on the phone last week leads me to the conclusion that your business is fundamentally sound. Business in general, and small business in particular, can sometimes have a mysterious ebb and flow to it. Since you are in a business without significant seasonal ups and downs, at first glance you might think the fault lies internally. Continue to monitor your progress, keep doing the things that have so far been successful. Take a hard look at projected expenses in the next quarter and see where you might cut back, without compromising on your marketing plans. If memory serves me, (and it's doing less serving and more searching lately) you have had almost nine quarters of growth since getting through your initial start-up struggles. As you know, I'm an advocate of growth through manageable change. It seems to me you have been doing just that. You've adjusted and tweaked ways of doing things as you've grown. You've branched out into other market sectors. Your service mix has been changed and don't forget you have taken on 14 full time people in just around three years of operating. That alone has created the need for changes including a move into larger facilities, a restructuring of your management team and redefining of your own role in the company. I think what you've hit are some speed bumps in your road, not the iceberg in your ocean.

Another thing you might look at are your sales and promotional strategies for the next quarter and see if there are any that could be improved. Remember, you can't expect to be an award winner in each category, so try matching the strategies to the strengths of your salespeople. I still believe your number one sales strategy is to make sure you are taking full advantage of your referral potential. Research has shown that customers often can't recall the competency level of a service provider when a time lapse as short as six months has occurred since they last had contact with the company. Make sure everyone is working their stay-in-touch lists, and remember to remind everyone to talk up referrals with their customers all the time. Maybe a quick referral generating contest would be fun and profitable about now.

This might also be a good time to hold a selling skills review for your salespeople. Go back to the basics. Remind everyone the foundation of your selling philosophy is to listen more, talk less, ask more and tell less. Remind them to be creative in adapting your service to the needs of potential and existing customers.

Are you still taking your public speaking course, and if so, how is it coming along? Did you know that in a recent survey of things people feared most, public speaking beat death three to one? Getting out and talking to groups about operating a successful small business using your own experiences can be a great promotional vehicle for your business. If you aren't doing it, maybe one of your salespeople could. Remember, all you need is a 20 minute talk.   Usually there is no shortage of clubs, organizations and associations looking for speakers to perk up their meetings.

I know you are a member of the local Chamber of Commerce and a couple of other business networking groups, but what about your salespeople? Make sure you encourage all of them to join one or two organizations they are interested in and prepared to be active in. It's important, however, to make sure they are joining for what they can bring, not just what they can take. Remind them to take the time to gain respect and develop rapport with people in the group before attempting to develop business liaisons.

Are you using or planning to use an direct mail promotion in the next quarter? Sending a mail-out to your current customers can be effective, but you need to measure the cost against the result. To make a mail-out successful, it must targeted to the right people. That's why it's so important to make sure your stay-in-touch list is updated at least once a year. It's your most effective list to use for direct mail. You can rent mailing lists from direct mail houses, but the response from those lists is likely to be significantly lower than the response you'll get from your own customer base. Keep in mind, what you mail is as important as who you mail to. If your entire yearly mail-out consists of newsletters, your customers may get bored with your mailing. Try mixing in some referral reminders, special service offers, or limited discounts to freshen up your mailing and keep it interesting. Don't forget the result of any direct mail campaign improves dramatically when you work it in tandem with personal or telephone follow up calls. Telemarketing can work if you call the right people and use the right format. In your business, a once-a-year call to all of your customers to survey them on their satisfaction with your service, need for additional service and possible referrals, can bring substantial results.

I've asked you to look closely at your marketing budget for the next quarter. Do you intend to do any print, radio or television advertising? Before you make your decision on media advertising ask for their reader, listener or viewer profile and match it against your target market. As you know, in your business, repeat advertising is likely to be necessary in order to have impact on your target market. Research shows that at least six repetitions of ads in your service sector are needed to make a lasting impression. There is no such thing as 'toe dipping' in advertising, you either have to take the plunge or stay out of the water.

Watch closely during the next quarter to make sure your business is not becoming frayed around the edges because of the almost continuous growth you've been going through. Get back to your core competencies and look for new and creative ways to apply them. And don't become so self-absorbed in problem-solving that you stop seeing the opportunities that are waiting to be discovered.

Doug

When your results are less than expected, the quality of your service must be examined and your examination should start with the person providing the service!

THE TEAM COMES TOGETHER

Dear Doug

We are on a war footing. No, not my phrase. It belongs to David who is one of our design coordinators. We decided to have a company wide meeting, bring everyone together and give them an insight into the growth of the company from day one, right up to our current situation. There are now 23 of us in total. We outlined our current situation to everyone. I explained that for the first time in our brief history we were not meeting our projections, sales were down and it appeared we might be losing market share. Our management team met a few days before the meeting to discuss our strategy, how we should conduct the meeting and how we should present the situation. We were divided on the issue of whether or not it would be productive to focus attention on the current business slowdown. I admit, I thought it would be too negative, but my opinion changed when I was reminded we had always prided ourselves on working as a team and keeping everyone in the loop. General consensus favored giving everyone an opportunity to know what was happening and that we should be candid in sharing our concerns. We also decided to have an open forum and encourage everyone to contribute ideas on how to improve the situation.

What a reaction it caused. I've read about groups of people and teams coming together in the face of adversity, but until that meeting I had never witnessed it first hand. During the meeting we gave everyone who wanted to an opportunity to speak. Let me tell you, the spirit of this team of coworkers is alive and well and has never been stronger. The people who spoke all voiced similar thoughts and opinions. We are in this together was the common theme. It turned out to be a great idea to share our concerns with everyone. Everyone pledged in their own way, that they and the team could and would do better. It became very apparent to me, the people in this company think of it not as mine, but as ours.

I'm sure you've already guessed, when it was my turn to speak, my voice was choked with emotion. All I could do was thank everyone for their support and make my commitment to do my part to get their company back on the right track. That meeting will always be one of the very special moments of my life. It was at the end of the meeting when David spoke, and at the end of his remarks used his war footing phrase. Everyone in the room stood and applauded. David's a pretty shy guy, and you should have seen the nervous grin on his face turn into a smile that would warm a January New England morning. We held the meeting ten days ago and you can feel, sense and see the increased energy level in the office. People have been more willing than ever to come forward with new ideas for cutting costs or improving operations. I'm now confident that we can manage through this downturn and that we will in the process remake an already competent team into an even better one.

Cheryl

COMMUNICATE
MORE EFFECTIVELY

Dear Cheryl,

What an incredible experience it must have been for you to see and feel the commitment of the people in your company. It was a very gutsy and unselfish decision on the part of your management team to want to 'tell it like it is'. I can only imagine the emotion that must have been sweeping over you during the meeting. You should be bottling and selling whatever mixture goes into your recruiting recipe. You sure have been able to attract some wonderful people to work with you. I would love to be there just to soak up some of the excess energy that must be bouncing through the office these days.

A few additional thoughts on how to continue to turn around the current situation. Ah, the loneliness of the long distance runner. No, I'm not writing to the wrong person and I haven't completely lost it yet. A lot of small businesses can be compared to runners in a marathon. Sometimes, in spite of your best intentions, you get a little ahead of your pace in the early going, so when you begin to tire and your pace slows down, it doesn't necessarily mean you're losing the race. You're marshaling your energy for the next push forward, at a more manageable and longer lasting pace. Based on your current situation, I would say you are in the middle of your race. Yes, things have slowed, but revenue is fine and everyone, including you, seems to have found new reserves of energy. It sounds like everyone is picking up the pace and a commitment to working smarter and more efficiently is in place. This unified sense of purpose can be a wonderful and fulfilling experience for everyone, just don't let people get so carried away they burn themselves out.

I think this would be an ideal time to have your management team work with their groups to help everyone sharpen their communication skills. Helping everyone in the company communicate more effectively with each other and your customers will pay dividends in terms of time, money and energy saved.

Communication between two people is always a three-way street. It consists of what one person thought they were saying, what the other thought they were hearing and what was actually being said. We've advanced from the cave to the $300,000 mortgage and been subjected to countless hours of psychological poking and probing, but we haven't been able to advance very far in terms of productive communication with each other. What used to be a grunt and a stick in the eye, has now become a memo and a knife in the back.

When communications breaks down, it can be nobody's fault, but in a small company, it can very quickly become everyone's problem. Human conditioning from the time of the caveman (oops, sorry - caveperson) comes into play. Their very survival depended on self-defense, closing ranks and keeping outsiders, like the occasional Saber Tooth tiger or woolly mammoth at bay. We've now evolved to the point where cooperation is the order of the day and working closely with others is necessary, if we're all going to reach our shared objectives. That means we might have to put ourselves at risk. It means opening up to others and sharing our thoughts, and emotions more openly with co-workers and customers.

The next time you find yourself having difficulty communicating positively with a member of your team or with a customer, consider these barriers to positive communicating.

We all live in unique and private worlds. Everyone one of us lives in a little world of our own as we grow up. We are the sum total of the unique experiences we encounter in our little world and we are influenced by the people, places and things that inhabit our world. We base our value system and our logic on what we learn from the life experiences we encounter growing up in our little world. Therefore, what one person considers logical and fair may not be according to someone else's life experiences. A discussion may go off the rails because one person can't see the logic in the others point of view or one persons value system is threatened by the other. A topic of conversation which for you could be something simple and mundane, could be very emotional and volatile to the person you are talking to. Why? Because of their past history and experience. Everyone at anytime may be receiving messages from both the heart and the head. Communications can break down when the balance between the two goes out of whack. Thinking with too much logic or too much emotion causes out-of-kilter communications. I mean, let's be honest, isn't Mr. Spock a real grain of sand in your shoe, sometimes? If during a conversation, you reject or dismiss a person's feelings, you risk making the person feel rejected.

We all have a certain degree of insecurity. We we are threatened, hurt or angry, we tend to let emotion override logic and we react with outpourings of blame and self defense. When are all very protective of our space in the workplace, so when we feel threatened there, our insecurities and emotions can bubble over very quickly.

This one may have escaped you in your rise from peon to boss. In conversations between two equals where one is more equal than the other, for example between employer / employee, there is a power imbalance. Open conversations often don't really take place in that setting. One person in the conversation may be influenced by a feeling of self-preservation, with the old, 'tell it like it is, as long as it's what she wants to hear' taking over.

Good communicating is more about having your ears open than your gums flapping. Even during a conversation concerning an important issue to you personally, it will be to everyone's advantage if you listen closely and explore the other person's point of view before you go off on your rant. You may be upset for the wrong reason. Remember there are three side to every story: yours, theirs and the actual. Too many times, when you are in a position of authority and under stress, the latter two are conveniently discounted.

When you find yourself in a situation where communication is breaking down, try defusing the issue by using some of these conversation bridges.

1. Can we back up a bit and take a moment to think about what has been said and make sure we understand each other?
2. Can we put a hold on trying to find a solution and just compare our points of view in more detail?
3. Go ahead and run your position by me again.
4. Let's take the first few minutes to get a little better understanding of where each of us is coming from on this one and then together try to figure out where the solution lies.

Take the immediate onus off solving the problem or finding a quick fix and start instead by trying to find a common ground. By trying first to achieve understanding you can reduce the emotion and competitiveness that can arise during conflicts of opinion. Under stress, people often have more interest in winning a discussion than in simply participating. Pretty soon the discussion becomes an argument. That's when logic and facts just start getting in the way of whatever people feel is important to them.

You can try to diffuse an argument in the making by acknowledging your vulnerability. Admitting your own vulnerability or fallibility can be very disarming to the person you are communicating with, and help ease the emotion and tension surrounding an argument. When you find yourself in a situation where a discussion is showing signs of becoming a full blown argument, and you will unless you are operating in a vacuum, try derailing the argument and getting the conversational train back on the track with the following comments.

1. I'm not sure I have the solution to this one, can you help me look at it from a different perspective.
2. Lets take some time to explain to each other where we're coming from on this one and what our real feelings are first.
3. I need your help on this one, I feel like I've lost perspective. Can you outline your position again, from a slightly different perspective, and help me understand?

Here's something worth thinking about. How often do people win an argument but walk away as the loser.

Doug

I personally believe we developed language because of our deep inner need to complain!

MAINTAINING MARKET SHARE

Dear Doug,

    I mentioned to you a couple of weeks ago, we had come very close to losing one of our major clients to a competitor. Competition is definitely heating up.

    When I started out and that was only as you know a little over three years ago, there really wasn't much competition offering the same type of service package I was. What I was doing was considered pretty unique in the marketplace. I should have known you can't keep a good idea hidden for long and that competition would be bound to increase, but now it seems like every time I talk to a client, they mention they've spoken to competitors I wasn't even aware existed. I think I know why its tempting to get into the business I'm in. Like a lot of service businesses it isn't expensive to start a business like mine. You can, as I proved, build this type of business from home, on your own.

    I envy manufacturers of expensive products, like cars, or planes or ships. I mean its pretty expensive to start your own car or plane or boat building business from the spare bedroom in your house. There is also a certain irony at work here. Even though we are a small business by anyone's standards, we have become the big player in our market niche. We are now the target a lot of home based start-up entrepreneurs go after. The good news is our client base remains for the most part, pretty loyal. The extra effort we've put in from day one building our reputation for quality service is paying dividends now. I know we have an edge on the competition because of it. However, we have had to spend some time just catching up on our knowledge of who the new competitors are and what they are offering. We are adjusting some of the services we are offering and I'm thinking of focusing more of our sales, marketing and advertising dollars and efforts in California. That's where we feel the most growth potential is for our services.

Cheryl

The brain is a wondrous thing. It starts working the minute we wake up and doesn't stop until we reach the office!

WHO ARE YOU REALLY
COMPETING WITH?

Dear Cheryl,

Don't fire me yet! I know I haven't responded to some of your recent letters but the book launch took more time and effort than I thought it would. The things a guy my age has to do to keep turning a buck! One of your letters made mention of increased competition. My response to that is - good. It shows me entrepreneurship is still growing. It also means you must be in a growth market sector where there is increased demand for the services your company offers. That's good new for you.

Imitation is the most sincere form of flattery, so you should be quite flattered. It seems everybody wants to be you. Isn't it great to be popular? It sounds like you're keeping a pretty close eye on what the competition is up to, and it's not likely they're going to have much of an impact on your market share. Keeping your eye on the competition is important, but be careful you aren't so busy watching the competition, you miss what's going on in the market. I'm sure you recognize this as a lead in for another learned dissertation on something, so in order not to disappoint you, here it is.

Being as much a sports nut as you are, I'm sure you will be able to relate very well to this little gem of wisdom. We work in a business climate where constant reference is made to being competitive, developing game plans and doing what it takes to beat the competition.

As much fun as turning business into a sport can be, it can be dangerously misleading. It suggests there is a well-defined, coherent game going on with established rules, level playing fields, referees and recognizable opponents with numbered sweaters emblazoned with their names on the backs. Not!!!

The sports analogy suggests that all it takes to win in business is to put together a better team than the other guy, then go out and beat him fair and square. Hmmm, sounds pretty straightforward to me. The problem with this is, in a climate of constant, and in fact, accelerating change, companies that set out exclusively to beat the recognized opposition, will at best, enjoy some short-term victories. The ultimate winners are companies who keep an eye on two things. The business sector they operate in and their immediate competitors. There is no point in being completely focused on beating the alligators in your swamp if the swamp is drying up. I'm not suggesting your competitors should be ignored, or not given due consideration. But your current competition is only critical to your future success if the game you are all playing is going to continue to be played in the future, by the same teams, using the same rules.

I like to use the example of a situation that occurred back in the old days, when I was in high school. Yes, I had to walk three miles a day to get there and it was uphill both ways. To get back to my story, I took what was then called the commercial business course. It was a course designed to give kids a good working knowledge of accounting systems, administrative systems and leading-edge business machines. Yes, I said business machines, not computers. Bill Gates hadn't been invented yet. In those days, the state of the art machines were electronic calculators. One of the dominant companies producing a machine that enjoyed huge market share was a company called Premier Business Machines.

When you went into any large accounting, billing or administration office you would see these marvels of high technology being put to use. All was well in the land of P.B.M. They were the dominant players in their market and their crack research and development teams kept turning out improved products every year. There was this one new little change to the rules of the game gaining some attention and recognition but it wasn't a direct competitor in the business machines field, so why worry. It wasn't even called a business machine or electronic calculator, it was called a computer.

Any competition for market share in the electronic calculator sector could kept at bay by new and improved P.B.M. calculators. The guys at P.B.M. were just about to dazzle the competition and the market place with the ultimate electronic calculator, when the market switched to computers. Too much focus on the competition, not enough on the market. Today about the only place you can see a state-of-the-art P.B.M. electronic calculator, is in a museum.

If that story didn't do it for you, try these on. How would you like to have been an exclusive manufacturer of expensive console radios, focused on taking market share from your competitors, when something called television came along. Or maybe the leading men's hat manufacturer turning out the best and most stylish men's hats, right up until the time men stopped wearing them? Remember, while the competition is staring you straight in the face, the real threat might be coming up behind you.

Doug

THE IMPACT OF GOALS AND OBJECTIVES

Dear Cheryl,

Thanks for sending along the bubbly for my birthday. The label indicates that your ever-expanding empire is able to provide you with a lifestyle you are having no trouble adapting to. You are proof that dreams can become reality for anyone willing to start working on theirs. I disagree with your assessment about having been lucky to find the right people to join your team. People like you work very hard at creating their own luck. As for your kind words about my part in the process, it has been minimal at best. In fact, the comments and questions contained in your letters have helped me greatly. I have been able to make changes in my seminars and keep them topical due in part to the fresh insights you have provided. This is important because it encourages companies to continue to pay me to conduct them. You know what a keen interest I have in generating revenue! Retirement? Are you kidding? Like you, I'm one of the lucky ones. I get to do what I love, have fun with it, meet lots of terrific people and get paid for it.

As requested, I'm enclosing my notes on the talk I give on the importance of setting objectives and goals. It's a good way to kick off the year, let me know what your people think of it.

At the beginning of a new year, each of us has a chance to sit back and take stock of our strengths and weaknesses. Even those with no apparent weaknesses, can sit back and take stock of their major and minor strengths. This is the time of year a lot of people start planning to have a better year than the one they've just completed. But planning alone won't make a difference, making plans to take action will. The beginning of any year offers us a great opportunity to look ahead. It's a luxury we won't have later. As we get deeper into the year, we become less proactive and more reactive. The pressure of daily living causes us to focus our attention on getting through today, or fixing what went wrong yesterday. There isn't a lot of time left for looking forward to tomorrow. It's the beginning of any year when the future shines brightest. It's when we declare "this year belongs to me, and I really mean it this time".

Your success in the coming year should not be governed by, or come as a result of, fate or a lucky break. It should come as a result of planning to take actions that will make you successful. Think of it as 'success by design'. Goals are the straw that stirs the drink, they help you mix your plans and actions together to achieve positive results. Use your goals as a benchmark to measure your performance throughout the year.

One result of working toward predetermined goals and objectives frequently overlooked is, it will cause you to have to be more proactive and less reactive in the way you live your life. When you establish goals, its easier to decide what's important and what isn't. You don't

Play to win, but play!

spend all your time on the small unimportant things, and you won't let yourself get bogged down in aimless negativity.

Instead you expend positive energy moving forward toward things that are important, and can make a difference in your life. Having realistic goals and combining them with a workable plan of action, can help you break out of any less than satisfying lifestyle you might be ensnared in.

Almost everybody finds it pretty easy to buy into the concept of setting goals. After all, how tough can it be to sit back and think up a bunch of goals and write them down. Not rocket science so far! But I don't really have to tell you, there's a bit more to it than that. It's not about sitting back and writing down goals, it's about getting up and taking action to reach them.

It's all about the change thing again. If you want better results, you've got to find a better way of doing what you do, or find something different to do. You aren't going to generate new or better results doing the same thing, the same way. In fact, if you haven't been reaching your goals, it's not because you're a failure. It's more likely because of the way you've been doing things. Success can be as close as changing what you're doing or how you're doing it.

Any goals you set need to be realistically attainable, given your experience, knowledge and skill set. The actions you take to reach them will be determined by your personal performance standards. You can't hope to reach high goals with low performance standards. Set your goals high enough to be a challenging motivational pull on your performance. But don't set them so high they create a daily environment of personal stress, anxiety or negativity.

The goals you set need to be clear, specific and detailed. When the Miss America contestant says, "My goal is world peace," the sentiment is laudable, but the feasibility is laughable. You need to be able to visualize your goals in realistic and workable terms. Be specific about what they are. You need to be able to see the goal or the reward, so that you can stretch yourself to get it.

Your goals need to stimulate you. They need to excite your senses and get those hormones out of cold storage and active again. One way to make goals more stimulating is to write them out and accompany them with interim rewards along the way, leading to a significant reward when you achieve each goal. Try using a descriptive, action-filled first-person account of what will be gained by reaching each goal. When you write them, put yourself in the picture. Write out a description of what life will be like once you've achieved your goals and how a typical day might unfold.

Your goals need to be agents of change. When you challenge yourself to reach for higher results and more difficult achievements, it becomes necessary to review your knowledge and skill set. In order to meet a more challenging standard of performance, you often need to improve your current skills or develop new ones. The improvement in your skill set will enable you to reach for even more challenging and rewarding goals in the future.

Keep your goals where you can see them. Carry your goals with you. Having them handy to refer to may give you the positive lift you need from time to time, when your universe is not unfolding as it should. Being able to refer to your goals often and easily has the effect of changing them from intangible thoughts into tangible commitments.

There is one last thing I would like you to think about in reference to goal setting and its the most valuable and overlooked aspect of the entire exercise. Setting our own goals is one step in the process of controlling the outcome of our own lives. It's a way to regain control of what we do today, and what we intend to do in our futures. A lot of people today live as Thoreau put it, "lives of quiet desperation." They don't feel in control of their future. Setting goals and objectives can play one small part in helping people regain a feeling of controlling their future and making a choice about the direction they want their lives to take. People who are not prepared to set their own goals and make the commitment to reach them, unwittingly find themselves spectators in the game of life, standing on the sidelines, watching success pass them by.

One final thought: make sure your staff are allowed to set their own goals, within company parameters. Goals that lack personal ownership, will also lack the commitment needed to attain them.

Doug

CHANGE IS …
THE 500 POUND GORILLA

Dear Cheryl,

I came away from our last phone conversation with the distinct feeling that you have become rejuvenated and ready to forge ahead with conviction and passion. You and your team did a masterful job of managing through your short lived downturn. I'm sure, as you said, the experience has left you with a more efficient operation and a more confident workforce. Pretty nice long term gains from a little short term pain, wouldn't you agree? You sound to me like you are ready, willing and able to look for some new worlds to conquer. Your comments about the incredible changes you've gone through really got me thinking about how unsettling change in the workplace can be for many people.

I believe one skill a small business entrepreneur needs to develop is the ability to work constructively within an environment of continuous change. Changes are always tough to deal with, but some are tougher than others. I think the line that establishes what our attitude to change is going to be, is the one that separates changes that are general to everyone and changes that are specific to us. General changes seem to be all right. They don't really bother us too much and for the most part they aren't seen as a threat to us. In fact if the general changes help make us happier or healthier, we embrace them. I think its safe to say, change that is general in nature and affects everyone, doesn't bother many and is accepted by most. When change gets in our face though, when it becomes personal and specific to us, especially in the workplace, a lot of people don't like it, so they either try to fight it or hide from it. Fighting with or hiding from change is not very productive. Change is like a 500 pound gorilla, running from it or hiding from it won't work, you've got to learn how to work with it.

During the last couple of decades hundreds of thousands of people made a scary but potentially rewarding change in their lives. They left the comfort of a real job, voluntarily or perhaps kicking and screaming, to enter the world of small business entrepreneurship. Hundreds of years ago, map makers used to paint dragons on their maps to indicate where the known world ended and the unexplored began. These unexplored areas were referred to simply as the land of the dragons. I'm sure, for many new entrepreneurs, setting up a small business must for them, feel like venturing into the lands of the dragons.

Entrepreneurs can't afford to fight with or hide from change. They've got to create it, adapt to it, and work with it. For small business entrepreneurs, seeking out change should be to them, what protecting the status quo is to big corporate business. I found a reprint of a newspaper article last year that I use in a lot of my presentations on change. I don't think I've shown it to you so I'll include it in this letter. I think it describes very accurately the way a lot of people are feeling about change in their lives today. It says, "Today, change seems like the only constant in most people's lives. Daily life seems to have become more dangerous and threatening and the world we live in has become more complicated and frantic. Expectations are higher and results are expected faster. We try to keep up, but just keeping up seems to take more of our time, our energy and our effort. Business and science race ahead at breakneck speed, heaping new discoveries on us so quickly that we stagger under the sheer weight of the volume. The one certainty we can count on is that the pressure to do more in less time will only increase in the years ahead." The really fascinating thing about this article is that it appeared in the Atlantic Journal in July-1837.

Changing what we do is very difficult and emotional, because for most of us, what we do is who we are. It's how we define ourselves and how others define us. Therefore, one of the first emotions we all have to deal with when we change what we do is our sense of loss. We are leaving behind familiar people, places and ways of doing things. It's as though we've shed our old skin but our new one doesn't fit just right, just yet. Its kind of funny though, when people look back they glamorize and romanticize the old days. We forget "the good old days" are the same ones we spent at least fifty percent of our time moaning and complaining about while we were living them. Here's one of my favorite quotes about change: "When faced with the choice between changing or proving there is no need to do so, almost everyone gets busy on the proof."

Doug

TAKING SOME PERSONAL TIME

Dear Doug,

    I trust you received and acted on my suggestions and revisions for the text of the speech you sent to me a couple of weeks ago. I love editing, it's such a control thing. I can't believe I've been operating my little business for almost four years. I'm not taking the time to look back though, - I'm too busy dealing with the *now* and *when* to think about the *then*. I am however, finally going to take some personal time and enroll in a few courses that really have nothing much to do with the business. I just have a desire to continue to learn, so the time off to take the courses is my reward for being a good entrepreneur, and having a profitable year. I'm planning to take a psychology course and, get this, a course in landscape gardening.

    Since we moved into the house, we've both taken a real keen interest in putting in a garden and I really enjoy getting my knees dirty on the weekends. But I'm getting a little tired of not knowing or remembering the names of the plants I'm working with. You know me I like to be on a first name basis with everyone and everything I talk to. No, I don't mean I give the plants names! You know what I mean. Weekends are becoming something both Rob and I are rediscovering. We have made a vow not to work during the weekends except for a couple of hours of preparation work on Sunday nights. What a wonderful, relaxing break they are! I don't know how I managed to force myself to work through so many of them in the last few years while getting the business started. Listen to me, I'm starting to sound like a veteran of the small business wars, and still just barely past my twenties, no comments necessary!! During the next couple of months, I plan to focus on encouraging everyone in the company to become more innovative and creative in their areas of responsibility.

I feel like we might be settling into a self-induced overly confident comfort zone and want to keep the entrepreneurial spirit alive. I'm also planning our first off-premises company conference in about four months. Part of which, is a two day weekend retreat. I would love to have you kick off the conference and do a workshop as well. That's if your schedule allows and my budget can handle it. Give me a call and we can negotiate.

Cheryl

THE INTANGIBLES
OF YOUR BUSINESS

Dear Cheryl,

Great idea to enroll yourself in the courses you described in one of your recent letters. The successful people I know never seem to stop learning. They continue to find courses and seminars to attend even after reaching what many people would see as a very high level of success. Naturally the courses they take vary according to their needs and skill sets. In your case, you don't need to add much to your knowledge of everyday business skills like sales, operations and administration. You have a good theoretical base and you certainly have added practical experience to the mix over the past four years. Your business has grown to the point where you have capable people helping you manage the primary aspects of it.

You now have the time, as you said, to just feed your need to know. You've been pretty focused on the everyday nuts and bolts of your business these past few years, and sometimes this creates a deficit in the ledger, on the soft skills side. This is a great time to improve your overall business competence, or more aptly put, your smarts.

Having smarts is not the same as being smart. A smart person, is defined by society largely as a person holding a degree. However, a good formal education does not necessarily make for a good entrepreneur. A small business entrepreneur needs to have a combination of book smarts, street smarts, theoretical intelligence, practical know-how, an intangible feel for business and people skills. Smarts should really be considered a small business core competency and they result from mixing business expertise with personal effectiveness. People with smarts are pragmatically creative. They know how to fly with eagles and when to scratch with chickens. Smart entrepreneurs are always open to new ideas and concepts, but their focus remains on the practical application of sound business principles, and the everyday needs of their business.

You can do some basic things, most having to do with the intangibles of operating your business, to make being in business more profitable and more personally satisfying. The first is, keep your eyes and mind open. Don't get so deep into the forest that you can't step back to admire the trees once in a while. Always be willing to look at change as an ally, not an enemy. Think of your operations as a giant cookie, get in there and experiment with the dough.

Next, don't just tolerate people, learn from them. There's lots of people out there with lots to offer. Know the field and the players on it. That means knowing your competition and your own people. Concentrate your attention on the 20 percent of the people, internally and externally, that make 80 percent of the action happen.

Finally, an entrepreneur should never stop learning. You must have an unquenchable thirst for knowledge and information. In this information-driven world, what you already know, even if it is more than most, is never enough.

One final thought. Take some time out of your busy schedule early in the morning or last thing at night, to just think. Thinking is an undervalued luxury in this world. Don't think about problems waiting to be solved, just think for the sheer joy of pondering the endless opportunities before you and the abundant absurdities surrounding you.

Doug

BEWARE THE DREADED COMPLACENCY

Dear Cheryl,

You're right, you need to start thinking about ways to keep the entrepreneurial spirit alive in your company. As companies grow and take on more employees, innovations have a tendency to get swallowed up by policy and procedure. People become accustomed to their way of doing things and change which was once something exciting and challenging becomes a pain in the butt. It sounds a little crazy to want to learn the steps to the change dance, just when you've perfected the moves to "it looks like we finally know what we're doing." But, as you so well know, one of the things I believe causes the decline of businesses is their penchant to plateau out and go into comfort zone maintenance modes.

One of the favorite business buzz phrases of the past was, "If it ain't broke, don't fix it." You still hear it once in a while today, touted by management dinosaurs. That simple phrase was responsible for more inertia and stagnation occurring in the workplace than almost all other factors combined. It was embraced and worshipped as business gospel by status quo advocates, business and government bureaucrats and creativity challenged managers everywhere. They repeated the phrase like some holy mantra, to defend well-entrenched 'let's do it like we always have' thinking.

You may not remember, but the phrase became a glib pop culture expression used by people who were basing their job security and corporate well-being on protecting and legitimizing the way things had been done, were being done, and would always be done. It didn't matter that the systems and techniques they were defending might be old, worn, faded and inefficient, or that they were inappropriate for the new workforce. What mattered most was that there was a sense of non-threatening familiarity about them.

Just image where we might be, or how we might get there, if the Wright brothers had embraced the 'if it ain't broke, don't fix it' philosophy. The bicycles they made were not broken, they sold well and they provided adequate transportation. They could pretty much take you where you wanted to go. No real reason to want to improve them. Certainly no reason to see if, by putting wings and a motor on one, it would fly. If it weren't for their entrepreneurial spirit, we might all still be looking up at the birds, wondering - how do they do that? Here's my answer to "if it ain't broke, don't fix it", "although the objective of reaching perfection in anything is unrealistic, the chase for perfection must never cease, because it's the chase that results in innovations and improvements."

Planned changes in your business should be a basic part of your business operating plan. There are few, if any, successful businesses operating today that are not changed through sales, marketing, operating, administrative, product or service improvements. One of the great advantages small business entrepreneurs have is they can respond to changing market conditions and consumer demands more quickly than the big guys. But you can't take advantage of new opportunities if all your time is spent focusing only on perfecting what you already know how to do.

If your business doesn't break from time to time, you aren't pushing it, experimenting with it or demanding enough from it. Adopting a business philosophy that embraces and searches out change will result in any number of advantages.

It will protect you and your business against complacency. It will put you in a position to react more quickly to changing market conditions. It will cause you, and others in your company to become more open to new ideas and opportunities.

The difference between success and failure for a lot of small businesses can sometimes be traced back to some very simple factors. Are the people running the business continuing to think creatively? Are the people running the business continuing to take action to apply creative ideas and innovations? Is everyone in the business continuing to commit to developing new skills?

In other words, are you encouraging everyone to think about how things are being done versus how things could be done? Are you taking the time to review creative ideas that might result in increased revenues or decreased costs? Successful businesses today stay healthy by feeding on creativity and the innovations that flow from it.

Big business has the luxury of solving a lot of problems by throwing money at them. They can use their financial clout to buy needed creativity. They can solve problems or create new revenue streams simply by buying up innovative companies and employing the creative teams that come with them. The high tech sector is a good example. Nice work, if you can get it. Small businesses, on the other hand, usually has to make up for lack of dollars by throwing home grown creativity at your problems.

When you're trying to encourage people to be innovative make sure you avoid the grim reapers that are always present when good ideas die.

Negative Attitude: Creative ideas won't have a chance to come to life, if you are looking at them with a negative attitude. They won't go far if you're always talking won't instead of will.

Cynical Outlook: The same applies if you are working with a cynical outlook. A cynical outlook is usually the result of listening too closely to uninformed people who offer you their opinions. Since these opinions are usually offered for free, you should remember that the value usually equals the price paid.

Nervous Anxiety: This can be a sure fire creative idea killer. Too much fear of failure leads you away from taking chances and back to the status quo. The only thing an entrepreneur should fear is losing the drive and determination to overcome the failures we all encounter from time to time.

Excessive Stress: Stress can impede the progress of any new idea or innovation. Don't try to make it happen all at once. In fact, you can make stress work for you when you learn to pace yourself. Work at implementing new ideas, in manageable increments.

Coloring Inside the Lines: It's great to be a team player and follow the rules, but following the rules and always coloring inside the lines can impede progress during any creative process. Think about bending, folding, mutilating, reshaping and breaking established rules. You can't do it the new way if you're thinking about it the old way. Remember, as Mark Twain said, "it is an advantage for those who think, to change their minds occasionally, and for those who don't, to at least rearrange their prejudices once in a while."

Spice it up, now and then!

That's it for now. Remember, you have no right to expect people working with you to think outside the box, if they see you spending all day in it, stapling the flaps shut around you.

Doug

THE NEW SUGGESTION BOX

Dear Doug,

We've implemented a system we hope will encourage everyone to look for and suggest changes that will result in making us more efficient and profitable. I guess it's a spin off from the old suggestion box. We decided to concentrate our efforts on one area of operation at a time so everyone could focus their thoughts on it together. The results have been very surprising and satisfying so far. What surprised me most was, a lot of good ideas have come from people thinking about operations outside of their immediate areas of expertise. It seems to be the macro versus micro view of things that enables people to see the obvious that's very often overlooked by the person directly involved.

We now hold a ninety minute 'change for the better' meeting every two weeks. Two people are invited to present their ideas at each meeting and discuss them with a committee of three others. The only two permanent committee members are myself and my operations manager. The other committee member is chosen from the area of operations being discussed. Doing it this way we hope to encourage everyone to take an active interest in the process. We're trying to give everyone a chance to participate. People coming forward with ideas, must be prepared to discuss their ideas in detail. They need to offer a reason why they feel we need the change, the reason the change will work, how it can be implemented and what specific benefits we can expect by adopting the idea. I'll keep you up to date on the progress we make and some of the ideas that we decide to implement. Everyone is very enthusiastic about getting involved and the process has uncovered a couple of good ideas already. It seems to have pumped a little of the entrepreneurial spirit back into the daily routine.

Cheryl

Knowledge - Skill - Action

A TRIP DOWN MEMORY LANE

Dear Cheryl,

You haven't heard this from me in a while, so here goes. I want to let you know, I'm very proud of what you've accomplished in both your business and personal life. Its often a real challenge and it can be very difficult for small business people to find the balance between a productive business life and a satisfying personal life. Let's tell it like it is. For a lot of small business entrepreneurs, life is spelled BUSINESS. That's what makes your accomplishments these past few years all the more impressive. There was Cheryl, just over four years ago, about to embark on the journey of her young life. You move to the other side of the country. You set up your one woman business, working out of your home office. Incidentally if ever anyone questions your optimism just show them pictures of your original home office, I doubt any further proof will be required.

Within two years, you're out into a real functioning business office, in an actual office building and have hired your first team members. Within a year of that move you make the next big move, into larger facilities or to use your phrase, 'world headquarters'. You now have over 20 employees, or team members, as you like to refer to them. You've branched out to provide commercial design services to many market sectors, and you're doing business in an ever expanding geographical area, including fifteen states and Western Canada. Now you tell me plans are afoot to expand again within the next 12 months. I believe if you'd been at Alexander's side, he could have cut his world conquering time in half. The most impressive part of all is, how you were able to find a terrific guy, juggle the time needed to let him dazzle you, then convince him to make the arrangement permanent. Maybe you should be writing articles on 'how to close the sale'.

As long as you continue to ask for my thoughts, opinions and ideas they're yours for the taking. I hope they'll continue to be a positive influence on both you and your team. Of course, there's another reason I'm happy to keep sharing my legendary expertise with you. It gives me a chance to take all the credit for your success, when I talk about you in my seminars. Even though we've covered a lot of ground these past four plus years, we've really just scratched the surface of what we can learn from each other. I thought you might get a kick out of my latest magazine article, I thought it might stir some funny and fond memories for you.

How Did I Get Myself Into This

Lack of challenge or creative license in their jobs may be what drives a lot of people to try setting up a business of their own. Others may have had the decision made for them after the boss used some creativity of his or her own. Know anyone who might have received a memo like this?

Dear Employee:

Even though we recently told you that your job was secure and your long-term future with this company was strong and full of life, we now find it necessary to declare you dead. Therefore, your future with us is terminated. Please arrange to have your body removed by the end of this working day. The Boss (at least for now).

Some people were driven to become their own bosses, because they were tired of hearing the daily corporate chant of "it won't work," "it's not your department," "its not in the budget." Whatever the reason, a lot of people find themselves waking up one morning and saying, "This is great, I'm the boss. Now what do I do?" What you do, is use your creativity to go out and get your piece of the pie in whatever business sector you choose to operate in.

Some people lose an opportunity to move forward and create a new life for themselves because their self esteem or self confidence is down a quart or they get talked out of putting their idea into practice by well meaning family and friends. Most of us have a tendency to doubt our creative ideas, so we often try to justify them by filtering them through what almost always turns out to be a negative process called "What do you think?"

- You begin the process by running your idea by a few acquaintances. They tell you they don't think it will work. That doesn't exactly give you the confidence boost you were hoping for.
- Stop asking the wrong people for uninformed opinions. If you have to get opinions, get them from people who know a little bit about what it is you're trying to do.
- You go from there to asking a few loyal and trusted friends, who also express misgivings about what you propose to do. Your friends are your friends for a reason. They like you. They don't want you taking risks since they want to protect you, and as most probably still have corporate jobs, they think you should be like them and get a real job too.
- If you are really desperate for approval, you go on to some members of your family. They tell you it might work, but they can't see how you can pull it off. What a surprise. You have just told them that you intend to become an entrepreneur, which the way they hear it, means you're never going to have a job again. Besides, when was the last time anyone in your family ever agreed on anything?
- Your research shows you everyone who is doing what you propose to do does it the same way, and it's not the way you intend to do it. Even the big guys all do it the same way, so obviously they must know what they're doing. Don't ever mistake bigness and sameness, for brightness.

Now, hopefully you have been able to ignore the unproductive negative filtering process you have put your idea through and are still determined to turn it into a practical, workable business opportunity. These are the next steps in the process:

Get Prepared. Lay the groundwork by gathering general information. Familiarize yourself with similar products or services. Solicit experienced, informed opinions.

Concentrate On It. Give your business idea the time and energy it deserves. Take time to think through all the aspects of turning the idea into a practical workable business. Make notes on the pros and cons.

Back Off For a While. Let the idea simmer, mull it over. Take time to turn it over to your subconscious mind. Visualize what your business will look like in its final form.

Evaluate It on a Small, Manageable Scale. Try a pilot project to test the business. Develop a check list for objective study of the results. Based on the results, decide to go ahead with your business, modify it, or scrap it.

I hope you enjoy this little trip down memory lane and get a few chuckles from it along the way.

Doug

RECOGNIZING ACHIEVEMENT

Dear Doug

I really got a kick out of your last letter and the jog down memory lane. Your article really did bring back a flood of memories. I remember so well running around getting anyone who would, to listen to my business idea and give me their opinion. Why my hairdressers opinion was so important to me, escapes me now. The reference to the family is right on the mark. The worst part was, they would tell me one on one they liked my idea, then I would hear from each of them that the others were just trying not to rain on my parade, great confidence boosters. The whole experience is pretty funny to look back on now, but it sure wasn't at the time.

On to more exciting issues. I knew you'd be excited when I called you to let you know about being honored by the Chamber of Commerce. Two days ago the newspaper had a nice group picture and article on all the winners of the 'Best Of Local Entrepreneurs' awards, and there I was front and center. Well third from the left actually, but still in the front row. I'm enclosing a copy with this letter. The awards dinner is really terrific, I've attended the last three, hoping but never imagining I would one day be a recipient.

Eight of us from the company will be attending the dinner, along with the members of my entrepreneurs alliance group. I told them I expect nothing less than thunderous prolonged applause and cheering when my name is called. The winners are asked to make a short two minute acceptance speech, which from my perspective is about one minute too long. I'm already getting nervous thinking about it, I know it's going to feel like the longest two minutes of my life.

Cheryl

The world's a stage, and most of us are desperately under rehearsed!

DON'T BE SURPRISED BY SUCCESS

Dear Cheryl,

I'm glad everything went so well at the awards dinner. I'm going to take you and Rob out for a little delayed celebration when I'm out at your conference next month. I think its very encouraging that your entrepreneurs alliance group is still going strong, after over four years, and with only one change in the group.

Your recent comments about how much you feel your self confidence has grown in the last few years are very interesting. We can all make self confidence as much a part of us as the sound of our voice or the color of our eyes.

It seems to me, when you look at successful people, they have a look of success. Let me explain. Successful people have the ability to always present themselves at their best, and at the same time, bring out the best in people around them. How do they do it? By having and using a 'most things are possible' attitude. To develop that look, we need to start by believing in our abilities. We need to take ownership and be responsible for our thoughts and behaviors. We need to be more selective about the thoughts we let in and the comments we let out. We need to spend more time mentally preparing ourselves to compete and succeed, by renewing our confidence reservoirs with images of ourselves as winners. We need to fill our minds with thoughts that are positive, realistic, and manageable, because they're all self-confidence boosters.

Self confident people expect to succeed and they aren't surprised by success. I've noticed that change in you over the last couple of years. In the early years you hoped for success and you were always pleased and surprised when it came your way. Now you plan for it and expect it. Part of the reason successful people become successful is because they begin with an attitude of can, and twin it with the skill to do. That's exactly what you did. The first thing a lot of people who want to be successful have to do, is raise their expectations of themselves. Confident people never set their sights too low. They never trap themselves into mediocrity by accepting the status quo. You've always demanded the most you could get from yourself.

Its a good idea for all of us to take stock of our personal achievement inventory once in a while. Most people have accomplished a lot more than they give themselves credit for. The best way to start your personal achievement inventory is by making a list of your business and personal successes, including both major and minor accomplishments, go right back to the time you won the three legged race at the school fair. Look back over the past year at challenging situations you handled well. Sit back with a nice relaxing glass of wine and think about things that turned out well, even though they might have caused you a lot of anxiety in the early going.

Let's look at some of the reasons for the steady growth in your self confidence since you started your business. You're now doing what you want to be doing, and doing it well. You're better at what you do than what you were doing, okay, you were pretty good then too, because you love it. It works this way, the more motivated you are to improve, the more competent you become, and the more competent you become the more confident you are.

Here's one a lot of people need to work on, including you. Lighten up a little. Compliment yourself and reward yourself more often. We are always ready to compliment everyone around us and feed them positive reinforcement. We need to look in the mirror once in a while and give ourselves a heaping helping of that positive reinforcement now and then.

Maintaining your self confidence isn't always easy, because, in spite of our best efforts to immunize ourselves against them, little self doubt bugs get into our system once in a while. They are kind of like flu bugs. Nobody goes out looking for them, they just seem to find us from time to time. Accept the fact that if you're going to make things happen you're going to question your actions once in a while. As long as you get over it quickly and don't wallow in it, it won't do you any lasting harm. The best way to avoid having self doubt sneak up on you too often is to face everyday challenges head on, stop wasting time worrying about them and spend more time doing something about them.

Doug

If you can't convince them, at least confuse them!

HOW THOUGHTS
INFLUENCE ACTIONS

Dear Cheryl,

I've had a chance to look over the agenda you faxed me. Your first full-fledged staff get-together off premises. It should be very exciting for everyone. Make sure you build in some fun and some free time. But listen to me, giving you advice on fun. You're the original party animal. Oh yes, I forgot, that was long before you became an entrepreneurial legend. It's going to be terrific participating as one of the guest speakers, and even more fun getting paid to be there. Remember, I offered to waive my fee. I was worried for a while, you might take me up on the offer.

I was going to say that it's hard to believe your business has grown to the point where it is, but you know, it really isn't so hard to believe. I know the work that you and your original hardy band of three have put into the business. It's nice to see nice people succeed, you and your group perpetuate the idea that cream always rises to the top. I'm including part of the text for the seminar I'll be giving your sales group in this letter, just to give you a little taste of what to expect. Give me a call and let me know what you think.

Some very deep thinkers over the past couple of decades have developed theories on why people of equal abilities don't always enjoy equal levels of success. Most of the theories share the following common thoughts:

What you think affects how you feel. All moods are created by thoughts. You feel the way you do right now because of the thoughts you are thinking at this moment. When you're feeling down, your thoughts will be dominated by negativity. Negative thoughts which cause emotional turmoil almost always contain gross distortions. Knowing how to overcome these distortions is important to everyone's well-being, but doubly important for people who generate their income from sales. If distortions caused by negative thoughts aren't controlled, they can result in increased selling resistance and selling anxiety.

They can, in fact, not only result in fewer sales, but also in less desire to sell. I refer to these distortions in my talks as "thoughts that go bump in the night" because thinking about them enough will scare the career right out of you. I'll list some of them here, along with their causes and cures.

Don't you understand! I'm right, you're not. This kind of thinking makes you continually defensive and the need to prove the correctness of your viewpoint becomes your sole conversational focus. An exchange of ideas should not be about winning or losing, or proving you're right and they're wrong. It should be about offering insights, expertise, information and opinions, with the understanding that your point of view is yours, and that others have theirs. You should be prepared to give the opinion of others the same respect you think yours deserve. Overcome this kind of thinking by genuinely listening to the reasons behind another point of view before deciding if yours is really the only possible right one.

It's not me! It's got to be them or it This kind of thinking leads to the need to find a scapegoat to be made responsible for your feelings, actions and results. You must accept responsibility for the results generated by how you think and act. The old adage, 'if it is to be, it is up to me', applies nicely here. You control your feelings and how you react to challenges and opportunities. Don't blame others for outcomes if your input could have been more constructive. At the same time, don't beat up on yourself for the outcome of situations you had no input into, or control over. Overcome this kind of thinking by looking less for someone or something to blame, and more for ways to help make things work.

It's all or nothing! This kind of thinking is referred to as polarization. It causes you to perceive things in extremes of black or white, with no shades of gray. Thinking like this can influence your opinion of your success and your ability, by making it necessary to win it all, at all costs. The feeling is, if you lose a little, you've lost it all. To get away from this kind of thinking, remind yourself that a piece of the pie is better than no pie at all. Try thinking in terms of a percentage of the whole, then be prepared to settle for your percentage.

I've got the crystal ball! You begin to think you have a unique talent for seeing into the future and you can tell how others are going to feel about your product or service even before you ask them. The problem is what you invariably see in your crystal ball is negative and leads to the 'why bother' syndrome. It starts with negative thoughts like, 'they'll never do business with me' or 'they'll never pay what I charge when they can get it cheaper from somebody else,' and ends with 'why bother calling them at all.' Get over this by concentrating only on what you do, or do not know, dealing only in facts and being objective. Don't get subjective about what if, what could have been, or what might have been.

I know what's fair! You think you're the only one that knows what's fair and you become resentful when others won't agree with you. Life is not fair. It never has been, never will be, so fair is not an option.

If you expect all situations to be resolved in a way you think is fair, you'll often feel disappointment. Frequently you'll feel hostility toward those you think made the unfair decision. Overcome this pattern of thinking by reminding yourself that in business, the client decides what's fair. You get to decide whether or not you want to play the game according to that set of rules. It's like that old twist on the golden rule: "Those with the gold, get to make the rules."

That's it for now. Remember, you'll always find more success dealing with people as they are, instead of the way you wished they were.

Doug

We don't like their sound and guitar music is on the way out. Decca Records memo rejecting The Beatles in 1962.

GETTING AWAY FROM IT ALL

Dear Doug,

First of all 'official' thanks again for helping make our conference such a success. Your cheque is in the mail. Ever heard that one before? It was fun seeing you 'in action' again. The sales people really enjoyed your talk and have responded with some new found enthusiasm, which I'm sure will pay off in additional sales throughout the year. No, you don't get a percentage!

Remember that real two week honeymoon Rob and I were going to go on a few months after our wedding? Well, two and a half years later, we're going. We're planning to get away for almost a month, that's two weeks interest on the two weeks we missed. Twenty-eight days in Australia and Southeast Asia. Rob is so excited about going home, to see his family and friends. I'm excited about going anywhere. I'm just kidding. I've always wanted to see all the places he talks about and describes so enthusiastically. It will be the first time we've seen his family since the wedding. You better be sitting down for this one. Rob is trying to convince me to consider a permanent move to Australia. He's already doing about a quarter of his business with clients there, through his web site on the Internet. He believes, and I might add is doing a fine job of convincing me, that the worst of the Asian flu is over and economies in that part of the world are on the rebound. He thinks the next decade will see incredible growth in tourism and business travel into that area. New hotels and restaurants will have to be built to cater to the influx of travelers. My business could be expanded to serve the area, or a new, separate venture could be set up. H'mmmm, the entrepreneurial blood is starting to heat up. Okay, it is a vacation, but a little poking around can't hurt, right? I'll drop you a couple of cards from exotic locations, just to rub it in a bit. Wish me luck.

Cheryl

A ship in the harbor is safe, but that's not what ships are built for!

ARE YOU LUCKY OR GOOD?

Dear Cheryl,

Congratulations, your great exalted entrepreneurship! A real holiday, proof positive that you are becoming one of the elite of the entrepreneurial world. A glorious 28 days, and in only your fifth year of operation. Amazing!

It sounds to me however, like there is more to this than a casual holiday and just a little poking around, as you put it. Do I sense a quest for new business opportunities in the making? I've been getting mixed signals from you during our last few conversations. You seem very positive about the business and your future expectations for it, but at the same time you sometimes seem wistful when talking about what changes and opportunities may lie in store for you. Anyway, I figure whatever comes as a result of the trip will be well thought out and whatever actions that are taken will be for the best.

I'm really pleased that you're taking more time to enjoy what you've worked so hard to build. You've earned it. You're a prime example of the old adage, the harder you work, the luckier you get. Its great that you describe yourself as being a lucky person, and indeed, if luck plays a part in creating a comfortable and interesting lifestyle, loving family, caring friends and a thriving business, then yes, I guess you are a very lucky person. But I think luck is a combination of looking for it, expecting it and doing something about it when you find it.

Have a great time, forget about business and have a Fosters or two for me.

Doug

Always do right, it will gratify some people and astonish the rest!

SEEING NEW OPPORTUNITIES

Dear Doug,

How can a month go by so quickly. When I was getting my shots for the trip I should have included one that would protect me against the entrepreneurial bug, because I think I got bitten. More about that later. What a fabulous vacation. We certainly kicked back and enjoyed ourselves. We were able to spend a two weeks with Rob's family and they threw what must have been a couple of tons of shrimp on the 'barby' for us while we were there. Did I mention the tanker truck or two of Foster's we drank to wash them down? What a wonderful time it was. My impression of Australia is that its the most Americanized country outside of Canada, I've ever been in. It has a great feel of newness about it and a prolific and growing small business sector, plus a real appreciation for individual accomplishment. It was like being in this very different, yet very familiar environment. I was very comfortable there and enjoyed the surroundings and the people.

We spent some time in Thailand. Wow, talk about exciting! The contrast between Bangkok and the villages in the countryside was mind boggling. It was like time traveling back and forth between centuries. What a difference between the delicate beauty of the quiet quaint villages and the crowded streets and manic pace of the capital city. Rob had some business to do in Singapore and Hong Kong so the rest of our time was divided between those two great city states. It was a fun combination of business and sight seeing. My lasting impression of Singapore is that of a thriving bustling city of gleaming glass towers. Hong Kong was incredible, it sweeps you up the minute you get there in the frantic pace of capitalism gone wild. Quite an experience.

The holiday was great, but its nice to be back in harness. I feel really physically and mentally refreshed and ready to go. As I mentioned when I called, Rob and I are really looking seriously at taking up residence in Australia. Rob was right, a lot of entrepreneurial opportunities are opening up throughout that part of the world and I would hate to miss them. For him it would be going home, and for me it would be another great adventure. His family and friends are a great bunch and I'm confident it wouldn't take long for me to adjust to my new environment. I've spent the last week talking to some of my multi-national clients about their operations in Asia and Australia and they had all the right answers. Most are already doing business there and others have plans to expand into the area within the next five years.

There will still be a lot of debate that will go on about whether or not we actually make the move. It would take at least six months or more to tie up the loose ends here. I want to do some extensive market research on the area before the final decision is made. I just wanted to share my thoughts with you at this point, in case you see a sale on sun screen.

Cheryl

EXPECT MORE AND GET MORE

Dear Cheryl,

If the enthusiasm in your voice when you called, combined with the excitement in your recent letter is any barometer, I think I can safely conclude that a good time was had by all on your trip. Nice to have you back in our part of the world, but for how long, I wonder? I forgot to mention it to you on the phone, I loved your cards. I have made note of your comments about moving or expanding your operations. The one thing I'm most confident in, is your decision making. Whatever you decide, it will be right. By the way, one of the great advantages of being at your age and your stage of the game, is that your skills are very portable. The older you get, the harder it gets to make life-altering or career-changing decisions. You and Rob haven't collected a lot of baggage at this point in your lives and careers, so use that to your advantage.

That was an interesting article you faxed me. You are absolutely right on the mark, when you say how much truth there is in it. You know, the gist of the article is really about the Pygmalion effect, from Shaw's book and known better to most people as the My Fair Lady effect, from the musical and movie of the same name.

Shaw's theory, later proven to be correct, claimed people's self image has a direct effect on their willingness to change and the results of their attempts to do it. Odd thing about human nature, people's accomplishments expand to fill their expectations of themselves. When we expand our expectations, we will increase the results we achieve.

For instance, when a low expectation level at work is allowed to exist, people's accomplishments will rise only to that level. If you want all your employees to be 100 percent predictable, and do no more or less than follow their job descriptions the result is bound to be average output and average results. They, and your company, will end up being consistently average. Average, by the way, is not something to aspire to. It's something people settle for because of circumstances which are often controlled by others.

Instilling higher personal expectation levels in people, then treating them as if they've become the person they need to be to reach those levels, will help them grow into that person. This encourages them to think and act differently, in order to meet the higher expectations.

The pygmalion theory:
1. First, must come a new self image, befitting the new, more successful you.
2. Next, positive thoughts and actions are needed to put you in a position to become more successful.
3. When the new you, created by your new self image, is combined with positive thoughts and actions, new levels of accomplishment will be reached.

In your mind's eye, perception is reality. If employees in a company perceive themselves as people doing nothing more than a no-brainer job, without potential for growth, they won't be looking for ways to show off their talents. If that perception is held by management, the employee's perception of themselves will be confirmed and they will act accordingly. When that company finds itself in need of clever, energetic, or adventurous employees, good luck. It's unlikely any of the people working in it are going to leap to their feet and volunteer to be that person. In all likelihood, they will remain quiet and everyone will miss another opportunity.

The good news is, self perception can be changed. Modifying and changing negative thinking and self defeating behaviors takes time and effort, but it can be done and the rewards far outweigh the time and effort expended to do it. Everyone has an internal voice mailbox. The first step in the process of building up your perception of yourself, is to begin leaving positive and challenging messages on your internal voice mail. Start reminding yourself that you have skills and you know how to apply them to get positive results. Set small interim goals for yourself and accept the challenge to go after them. Remember, you can choose your own perspective on how you respond to challenging situations. You can convince yourself you're a failure and by doing that be sure to fail. Or you can convince yourself you can succeed and end up doing it. What have you got to loose? Trying to succeed is always more fun than giving in to failure.

Let me sum it up this way. Anyone can raise their personal performance level, by building a positive perception of themselves and combining it with a positive attitude and positive actions. It's always been troubling to me that so much of what is written and talked about in reference to positive attitude seems to ignore reality. Much of it is very inspirational, but you begin to get the idea that positive attitude in and of itself is all you need to guarantee positive results. It won't, because it's not enough. A positive attitude will have an impact on the way you communicate, and on the relationships that are important to you. It can make you happier and healthier. It can make you a better butcher, baker or candlestick maker but only if it is combined with talent, knowledge, skills, drive and determination. Having a positive attitude is more than blithely smiling while the world around you crumbles at your feet. Its not about ignoring negative situations and trying to will them away or convincing yourself all is well when it isn't. Positive attitude is about finding the strength to deal with challenging situations around you and taking the appropriate actions necessary to generate positive results. Significant challenges in your business and personal life won't go away until you pair the right mind set with the appropriate actions. Positive self perception and attitude plus positive actions equal positive results. A positive outlook gives you the confidence to put yourself at risk more often. The greater the risk, the greater the reward.

Doug

COME SEE ME SHAKE

Dear Doug,

    Just a quick note to tell you I'm making my first big foray into your area of expertise next month. I've been invited to be one of the speakers this year at the annual conference of commercial interior designers. I'm told there will be about four hundred people at my session.

    What is it about public speaking that scares, no, make that terrifies me and everyone else I know, so much? I asked the group at the last entrepreneurs alliance meeting how they felt about making a speech to a large audience. The results of the poll are as follows; two said they would prefer death, two said they would rather go out on a blind date and one just ran screaming from the room.

    I'm always very self assured in smaller groups and I don't need to tell you how much I enjoy the spotlight and being the center of attention. But when it comes to giving a speech to a large group, well, my knees begin to quiver just thinking about it. I'm afraid the people I'm talking to will be able to hear the terror in my voice or that my voice will start to squeak, as my throat dries up. Will they, I wonder, see the nervous twitch in my left eye from where they are sitting? I'm sure I'll break out in enough sweat to rival a breach in the Hoover Dam. I'm starting to get other invitations to speak at various events and I would like to do more in the future, but not if the toll taken on my nerves remains this high. HELP !!

Cheryl

GET THE BUTTERFLIES
INTO FORMATION

Dear Cheryl,

Well, yet another new talent is uncovered. I'm sure your speech will dazzle the audience. I'll be very surprised if you don't come away with a desire to do more, once you get the first one under your belt. It's pretty heady stuff, getting up in front of all those people and having them listen to your message. I can relate to the "butterflies." I still get them after 20 years. A friend once gave me a piece of advice about stage anxiety. He said, "You'll never get rid of the butterflies, the best you can do is, try to get them to fly in formation". The point he was making of course, was that you should work with your anxiety to give yourself the stage edge and energy you need for a good performance. For what it's worth, here are some tips from an old professional gum-flapper.

Carry a positive attitude with you when you get up there. Just the thought of public speaking inspires more fear and trepidation in most people than it should. I'm sure part of everyone's concern is, they might put on a poor show and have lots of people witness it. This is the point where anxiety can become full-fledged stage fright. To keep your anxiety at a manageable level, remind yourself you've been invited to speak because people are interested in what you have to say. They're looking forward to enjoying your talk, not watching you fail. They are not sitting in judgment, they are sitting with anticipation and they want you to succeed.

Tell them what you know. That sounds pretty basic, but too often, for whatever reason, people take on a subject they know little or nothing about, and it shows. Stick to your knitting. You know a lot about running a successful small business and about the issues and concerns of small business entrepreneurs, so you won't run out of things to say. Incidentally, try using this formula for delivering your talk. Tell the audience what you're going to tell them, go ahead and tell them, then tell them what it was you told them.

Show them your energy. You're pumped so show it. Don't be afraid to put some show into your tell. Speak with enthusiasm and passion. Get physical, use gestures to punctuate key points and be animated. This makes the presentation more visually exciting for the audience. The audience will see you as a more dynamic speaker and you will capture more of their attention. Be careful though, to match the size of your gestures and your energy level to the size of the audience.

Look 'em in the eye. Pick out some members of the audience and make eye contact with them. Hold it for short periods of time, as you would in any personal conversation. Slowly sweep your gaze from side to side, to keep everyone involved, but be careful not to get your head going back and forth like you're watching a tennis match.

I usually takes about three weeks to prepare a good off the cuff speech.

Be a speaker, not a reader. Speak from the heart or speak from key word prompts. Don't read from a prepared text. If you want to do that, why not just mail everyone a copy of your speech and let them read it at their leisure. Let the audience see you. Use the lectern to keep your key word prompts on and to refer to from time to time, but let people see you.

Rehearse to look off-the-cuff. Always practice your presentation as many times as it takes to make it look natural and unrehearsed. After a few times through it, time it out and put time indicators beside some of the key words to help keep you on pace. I hope these little hints help you deliver the dynamic presentation you're capable of and I hope you enjoy the butterfly net I'm sending you.

Doug

MAKING A POSITIVE IMPRESSION

Dear Cheryl,

I thought these suggestions for making positive impressions might come in handy at the next meeting you have with your sales team. We all know the importance of positive impressions, especially the first one. In fact, the first one better be good or its likely to be your last one. Impressions are formed by people first, on the basis of seeing what's on the outside and from that, making assumptions about what's on the inside. This isn't always fair, but its always the way it is. People assume very quickly, what they see is what they get. You have to establish value and credibility in what they see and you need to do it quickly.

Don't waste the only chance you may get to make a positive impression on someone by not being on top of your game physically, mentally and emotionally the first time you meet them. The effort you need to expend to make a favorable first impression is significantly less than the effort you will need to put forth in order to undo an unfavorable one. Ensure that the impressions you make count. Determine what impression you want to make in a specific situation and decide what you need to do, or avoid doing, in order to make that impression.

I have included some guidelines you might want to pass along to your salespeople to help them make favorable first impressions during a sales call.

1. Use your physical presence positively. People believe and remember what they see. Use positive body language. Stand and sit straight, make eye contact when listening and speaking.
2. Make purposeful motions when presenting sales materials, product samples and the like. Place a value on what you are handling by treating it with respect and present it with a purpose.
3. Show people what you mean by coordinating your words and your actions. As much as 75 percent of what people absorb during a conversation or presentation is transmitted non-verbally.
4. Be flexible in how you communicate with others. No one style is effective with everyone, every time. Try to match your method of communication to the person you are communicating with. You don't have to change your personality or become phony, just make some slight adjustments in things like the speed of your speech, the volume or tone.

Doug

ASKING THE RIGHT QUESTIONS

Dear Cheryl,

Consider this as part two of the how to make a good impression series. It's all in what you ask for, and how you ask for it. The reason a lot of salespeople walk away from a good selling opportunity, frustrated and without doing any business, is because they're asking the wrong questions, the wrong way, at the wrong time.

Most active conversations involve a lot of questions and answers. Questions can be used to create connections and make people feel part of the decision-making process. Questions can be used to get people involved, they create opportunities for people to claim ownership of ideas and bond with each other. You can use questions to buy time in critical situations. The time it takes for others to respond to a question can give you breathing space and time to alter your course of action, if necessary.

Questions, such as, "would you like to begin with your point of view" can be used to start positive conversations. Questions can also be used to sum up conversations on a positive note, such as, "have we covered everything to your satisfaction?" In almost any sales situation, most of what the salesperson needs to know can be discovered by asking some or all of the following questions:

1. How can I help you?
2. How soon do you need it?
3. Are you confident our product / service will fill your need?
4. Is there any other information you need before deciding to do business with me?
5. Is there anyone else I should talk to?
6. When will your decision be made?

Please don't think I am advocating asking the previous questions in rapid fire sequence, under a bright light, while wielding a rubber hose. Each of the questions, should be asked in the salesperson's way, used at the appropriate time and in the appropriate way. Questions should always be asked in a way that invites a friendly response. The voice and attitude of the person asking, should convey friendly interest.

Make questions conversational in nature. Use follow-up questions to help the other person expand on their responses. Ask your question, comment on the reply and encourage further dialogue with comments like: "That's very interesting, could you tell me more about it" or "Please continue, I'm learning a lot."

Avoid asking trick questions or waging probing attacks. Remember, you're trying to have a conversation, not win a conversational contest. Questions that every salesperson should be dropped through a trap door for using include, "Why on earth would you do that?" "What made you think I would agree to that?" and "I'm sure you would agree that my idea is better." The only thing missing from those questions is to add "bozo" at the end of each.

The final, and most important, element of questioning, to consider has nothing to do with the question, or how you ask it. It has to do with the reason you ask questions in the first place, which is to hear answers. You can't hear unless you listen. If you aren't prepared to listen carefully, don't bother asking. A good sales presentation is about having a conversation, not conducting an interrogation.

Doug

THE WAITERS AND THE DOERS

Dear Doug,

We are having an outstanding year, sales and profits are up nicely and everyone should be very happy with their profit sharing cheques this year. I forgot to mention on the phone last week, I've accepted an invitation to speak at the Business Advisory Councils' Awards Dinner being held in Portland in two weeks. I'm enclosing a copy of my speech. You were right, since I got that first big speech under my belt at the conference a couple of months ago, I've been looking forward to the next one. I thought in my speech this time, I would try to summarize what I've learned, what you've taught me, and how I feel about small business entrepreneurship. You might find it a little emotional in places. I decided if I was going to do this talk, it would be from my heart. Writing it brought a lot of the feelings that I have been having lately to the surface. Let me know what you think of the speech. You may notice that I have borrowed a few thoughts from your seminars and tapes. I think borrowed sounds so much nicer than stolen, don't you?

"Entrepreneurship is a way of getting the most out of who we are. When we first begin to think of ourselves as entrepreneurs, it changes our way of looking at things. It begins to reshape old patterns of behavior and ways of doing things. It adds excitement and challenge to our lives.

Real entrepreneurs are children in adults bodies. We have a childlike ability to dream real dreams again. We can imagine the unimaginable and are convinced we can make the impossible become possible. After all we were able to talk the bank into a start-up loan, weren't we!

The great thing about starting your own business is that not only do you get a chance to be the boss, you get a chance to start over. You get a chance at another life. You can if you want, throw out the old you, and become the new you. What you did or didn't do, who you were or weren't, what you thought or didn't think before you became an entrepreneur and started your business, is old news. What matters now is, do you have the drive and determination to overcome the inevitable challenges and obstacles you're going to face on your way to becoming the person and the success you want to be.

If you were a success in a job, working for someone else. Chances are pretty good you already possess the knowledge, talent, skills and attitude you need to be a bigger success working for yourself. The main difference is, now you're in the captain's chair, you have control, you have the power to make the decisions that will determine your success or failure. You control the level of your income, your achievements and your satisfaction. But let me tell you that captain's chair can sometimes turn into a hot seat.

When you think about the skills needed to run a successful small business today, the mind begins to boggle. You need to be a manager, a motivator, an administrator, a financial expert, a salesperson, a marketing specialist, a psychologist, and a computer whiz to name only a few. The myriad of skills you need to have should lay to rest the myth of the natural born entrepreneur. Successful entrepreneurs today are made, not born.

Success in business today demands a willingness to be flexible in how we use our talents and how we display our attitude. Keep in mind that everyone of us is first and foremost in the people business, (I know the techies among you are working day and night to overcome this apparent glitch in an otherwise perfect world, but until the breakthrough comes, people are what business is about). How we communicate with our customers and employees, the attitude we show toward them and the actions we take with them, will determine our level of success. It is an established fact that, with the exception of politicians, thoughts precede actions. Generating positive thoughts about who you are and what you do, will generate positive actions and result in positive accomplishments.

Starting a business provides you with the opportunity to succeed. Whether or not you turn that opportunity into success depends on understanding, accepting and working with a few simple and not very trendy concepts and realities. You need to have an old fashioned work ethic. You need to be willing to do what needs to be done, when it needs doing. Think of it this way, there may be competitors who are smarter than you, some who have more skills, others who have more connections, lots who have more capital, and even a few who may be better looking. You can't do much about that. But fortunately for those of us who are less gifted, not as skilled, connections challenged, short of money and plain to a fault, there is one great equalizer. We can outwork the competition. The surest way to breathe life into a new business is to go out and find customers for your product or service. How? By working hard, working consistently, and working effectively. By making things that have worked for others, work for us. By doing things differently, or doing different things. Or by doing what we've always done, only doing it better and more often. When a business fails its not because the people behind it are failures. A business fails because of how things are being done. What's really frustrating and sad is that most of the time those businesses could have been saved by simply changing the way things were being done.

It's not easy running your own business. Its difficult to beat the odds and build a successful business. Its difficult to repeat success from one year to the next and some success doesn't guarantee a lot of success. There are some things you can do, however, that will improve your chances of building lasting success. You have to build on a solid foundation of positive business principles. Have a keen interest in making sure your customers are treated fairly because small business grows through the words of satisfied customers. You can maintain steady growth by doing business the right way. Make doing what's right, your choice not your obligation.

I think people can be divided into two distinct categories. No, not those on the Internet and those who aren't. I'm talking about the waiters and the doers of the world. Waiters you can probably guess, are people who just wait. The one thing they do better than anything else is wait. They have waiting down to a science. Waiting is what they enjoy most. Eventually it becomes their mission in life. They wait for a break. They wait to be successful. They end up waiting all their lives for life to begin. Doers like us can't wait, we've got too much to do."

Cheryl.

The time you spend thinking of ways to impress your peers, would be better spent accomplishing what they are likely to be impressed by!

THREE ENTREPRENEURIAL MYTHS

Dear Cheryl,

Thanks for the call to let me know how your speech went. I knew from reading the text, it would be terrific. I'm sure everyone was inspired by it and found something in it that will give them pause to reflect positively on their own situation. I really enjoyed the description of the waiters at the end of the speech. I've known a few myself along the way.

It was very clear in your speech and our conversation last week how strong your emotional attachment to small business entrepreneurs is. I'm going to expand on my feelings about entrepreneurs in this letter by discussing some of the myths associated with them. Entrepreneurs in some ways have been misrepresented and misunderstood. Let me lay some entrepreneurial myths to rest once and for all.

1. Entrepreneurs are high-risk takers and the riverboat gamblers of business waterways. Wrong! They are risk-takers, but so is everyone who eats fried food, remember Elvis. Entrepreneurs are prudent risk-takers. What, you might, ask is a prudent risk-taker? It is someone who takes action only when an acceptable risk/return ratio has been established.

2. Entrepreneurs are blue sky painters and idea people, not capable of implementing their ideas. Wrong! Entrepreneurs do the grunt work too. They figure out how to negotiate the curves and overcome the challenges of getting a new idea accepted and

launched. There is a big difference between people who simply have ideas, and entrepreneurs who put ideas to work.

3. Entrepreneurial ideas are the result of blinding flashes of brilliance. Not likely! Ray Kroc founder of McDonald's wasn't struck from out of the blue with a vision of golden arches. He had the entrepreneur's eye for unique opportunities and saw his in the way the McDonald brothers operated their hamburger stand. He also had the entrepreneurial sense to seize the opportunity and make something of it.

Doug

Only those who are willing to fail greatly, can ever hope to achieve greatly!

THE CAPTIVE ENTREPRENEUR

Dear Doug,

What is the average life span of the captive entrepreneur? It seems to me that we don't live long when captured and chained to everyday tasks. When I look back at the last two and a half years and compare them with the early years, I realize I have become, out of necessity, more management-bound and less entrepreneurially-free.

The real irony in the situation is, our commitment to providing an entrepreneurial friendly environment has enabled us to attract and keep talented and highly motivated employees at every level. I still love the business and the people who work with me. I just don't like a lot of the things I have to spend my time doing. I don't feel as free to create and innovate as I used to. All my time seems to be taken up with management issues. There always seems to be more at stake in every decision. There seem to be more angles to look at than ever before.

My head tells me I built this company so I would have a long-term, successful business to operate. My heart tells me I still love what I do, but I'm not in love with doing it anymore. I told you when we returned from our trip, I was intrigued with the idea of setting up shop in that part of the world. Rob and I have continued to talk about it since then and maybe I'm just looking for a convenient reason to move on.

Rob and I have put together plan B. It involves selling the company, hopefully to some of the people who have helped me make it successful. We will then make the move to Australia, settle in and launch a new smaller version of what I did here. Rob will work with me in the new company, so you know its going to be kept small and easily manageable. We considered the possibility of setting up the overseas operations as part of the existing company, but that would just mean an even bigger and more bureaucratic operation to manage.

No final decision has been made, but I have told the people here about the possibility of selling and leaving, and I'm working on a financing package to help a group of them buy the company, if and when the time comes. You know me though. I'm not about to delay the decision one way or the other for very long. I can't help thinking I'm letting some of the people who came to work with me down. I'm supposed to be their leader, and here I am planning to leave instead of lead. I'm going to close now, writing this to you has made everything seem much more real and much closer than I had allowed myself to think it might be.

Cheryl

WHAT IS LEADERSHIP?

Dear Cheryl,

So you think your management responsibilities are squeezing the entrepreneur out of you. Never, you're a dyed-in-the-wool entrepreneur. This has more to do with the entrepreneurial bug biting you on your trip than the rigors of managing the company. If it were just about your management duties you could hire or promote someone to be in charge, and you could step back into an advisory role.

I wouldn't be questioning your leadership if I were you. I've always believed that you are a great leader. If you're starting to have thoughts about selling your business, reflect on some of the ideas and concepts we've shared over the years and be guided by the collective vision that you and Rob share for your future.

Let me explain why I have always admired your leadership. You are not like a lot of typical leaders, who lead only by virtue of being in the lead role. Some people lead by position, they think leader is spelled B O S S. Leadership is about doing, not being, and you've always led by example. Remember when you were the one managing the business Monday to Friday, then bringing in your vacuum to clean the office on Saturdays?

The quality of the actions you initiate and the results they generate define your leadership. I like what Eisenhower is quoted as saying about leadership, *"Until and unless you can get someone to do what you want done, when you want it done, the way you want it done, because that someone wants to do it, you may be in charge, or you may be a manager, but you aren't a leader."*

As a leader, you have been able to use your own drive and determination to inspire others to accomplish more than they believed possible. In many ways, you and your organization epitomize what overachieving is all about. You've demonstrated how a group of diverse talents can be brought together and become much stronger as a team, than they were as individuals. You sold people on your vision of what the company could be and the single most powerful force for bringing people together is an ongoing commitment to a shared vision. If your vision of the companys' future and your role in it has become clouded by uncertainty, its going to affect your ability to lead and manage those around you.

Managing is about concentrating on the process of getting things done through people. Leadership is about concentrating on the people who make the process work. George Bernard Shaw said, "Leaders are great believers in circumstances, if they don't find the circumstances they want, they change them." It may be time for you to take old George's advice.

I guess the best way to sum this up is to say that managers, for the most part, work toward achieving goals and objectives. Leaders work toward achieving visions. The true value of a vision lies not in what it is, but in what it makes you want to do.

Doug

OPENING A NEW DOOR

Dear Doug,

I sat down early this morning to try to come to grips with the reality of our decision. I knew before I called you last night, it was going to be a long and very emotional conversation. Needless to say, I didn't get much sleep last night rehashing our talk. Thanks again for the supportive and encouraging words. I really needed them. The decision to sell and move on looks the same in the light of a new day as it did when Rob and I made it yesterday. I know its right and I know its time, but for a lot of reasons it doesn't make it any easier. I never thought when the decision was made it would be so unnerving. Even during our negotiations to sell the business to my management team, it didn't somehow seem real. I guess I couldn't bring myself to face the actual thought of selling and leaving.

I'm riding the emotional teeter-totter again, sad at the thought of what I'm leaving and incredibly excited about where I'm going. When I think about the new challenges, opportunities and surroundings I'm heading for I get a surge of can't wait to get there. Then I think about what I've built here and the people who helped me build it, and back down I come. You and Rob are the two people who understand most what an emotional parting this is going to be. Its really not selling the business that's upsetting, we have profited very nicely from the sale. It's leaving the people. You said once, we're all first and foremost in the people business, and these people were my business. I'm not even sure how long its going to take me to finish this letter. I've had to stop three times, wipe the tears and gather my thoughts.

It should take about ninety days to wrap everything up and be on our way. We're planning to come back east next month to say goodbye to everyone, so I'll see you before we go. I'd like to spend some quiet time with you if possible. Maybe we could sit for an afternoon, at the corner table in the wine bar at Jonathan's, and philosophize. I'm also putting you on notice to be ready for the goodbye party of the century. There will be a lot of laughter and for sure, a few tears. It'll be the first time I've seen a lot of my old friends since I left to come out here, and once again it's to say goodbye.

My fingers are shaking as I type this and I just feel so damn sad. Why does there always have to be roses and thorns to everything we do? In so many ways, Rob and I are excited about starting a new life in Australia, surrounded by the friends and family he left almost ten years ago. Yet, in the last few days, we've both admitted to being very sad and introspective about leaving the family and friends we have here. It's been almost twelve years since my Dad died and yet, at times like this, I still just want to reach out to him for a hug.

I still have every letter you've sent me over the years. I've never told you how many times, in the early years, I read and re-read them. Not just for what was on the lines, but for how you made me think about what was between them. They were sometimes clever and full of wisdom, often times plain and simple, most times funny and interesting and dare I say it, occasionally pretty dull. But you weren't writing to impress me, you were sharing your expertise, thoughts, feelings and emotions with me. For that I am, and always will be more grateful than you can ever know. In some ways, I'm glad I got to know you from a distance. Up close, I'm not sure you or I would have been as candid or ready to open ourselves up the way we have. You have been much more than a mentor and advisor to me. You have been my confidant and true friend. See you in a couple of weeks. You can be sure, when the good-byes are said and its time to go, I'll walk away looking forward toward my future, just the way you taught me to.

Cheryl

LIVING AND LEARNING

Dear Cheryl,

"Now, this is not the end. It is not even the beginning of the end. But it is, perhaps, the end of the beginning." I always love quoting Winston Churchill. He's the short rotund guy smoking the big cigars and holding up his fingers in a V sign, you see in those black-and-white newsreels from the Second World War. I can't say your decision to sell your business comes as a surprise. It's the entrepreneurial elf coming out in you again. I would be less than honest though, if I didn't say I was going to miss both you and these letters.

What I thought was going to be a simple exchange of thoughts, ideas and concepts, has really become part of my life. You're on your own next time, and in fact, I'm hoping somewhere in the future you'll develop a similar relationship to the one we've enjoyed, with another budding entrepreneur. It's been a pretty interesting chapter in both our lives, wouldn't you say? I think back to when we met. It seems only a few short years ago that you hired me to conduct seminars on managing change for the company that employed you at the time. Little did I realize that you were actually listening to what I was saying.

How could we have imagined, you would have to leave that company and strike out on your own? Or that you would move to the other side of the country. We certainly couldn't have imagined what a great chapter of your life would be written there. I recall our early letters and when I look back at them, (yes, I still have them), I can sense the apprehension and anxiety, mixed with the excitement and confidence of the budding entrepreneur. I remember how over those years, we brainstormed through our letters and I recall the small, hesitant growth steps you took in the beginning, like a baby learning to walk.

I remember when you proudly declared, "It's time to move out of the home office!" You were out and moving up. Then the big move a couple of years later, from the small office to 'world headquarters'. I recall how you went through those first few months trying to keep the self-doubt and anxiety from seeping in through the cracks in your confidence. Then the heady months of good times and growth. The hiring of your first three people, Beth, Tom and Karen, how they stayed with you and rode the roller coaster at your side all the way. I sure get a kick out of the idea that they're part of the management who bought the company.

Remember the first short downturn you went through and the angst you suffered over whether sales were falling because of what you were doing, or in spite of what you were doing? How you earned what I call, your real life degree in management, during those two tough quarters. You did what I knew you would, you changed what needed to be changed, rekindled enthusiasm and came back at the market smarter and stronger than ever. Since then it's been almost non-stop and well-managed growth.

The company you created with your vision, values, dollars and sense is now a well-respected market leader. One very significant and memorable milestone came when you were finally able to justify my exorbitant rates and bring me out to conduct a seminar for your employees. A lot of emotions rolled over me when I thought of what had come to pass for both of us, since the last time you had participated in one of my seminars.

Let's not forget the personal changes as well. Your marriage to Rob - what a great guy. Anyone who lets me beat him at golf will always be all right with me. The wonderful lifestyle you've created. I salute you, Cheryl, as a person, a business woman, an entrepreneur and a friend. I said when we embarked on this journey that we would do it as equals, so let me sum up my feelings with this thought. While we are busy teaching our children all about life, our children are busy showing us what life is all about.

Doug

Timing has a lot to do with the success of a rain dance!

WE LIVE AND LEARN

When we live with an open mind,
we learn to admire what is different
When we live with clear goals,
we learn to move forward.
When we live with recognition,
we learn how to win.
When we live as leaders,
we learn how to inspire others.
When we live with a sense of humour,
we learn how to enjoy.
When we live with self-worth,
we learn the value of others.
When we live with self-confidence,
we learn to admire others.
When we live with tranquillity,
we learn to appreciate the things around us.
When we live with imagination,
we learn there are no limits.
When we live with determination,
we learn to overcome.
When we live with love,
we learn to be free.

Adapted from "Children Learn What They Live"
Dorothy Law Nolte

SPEAKERS FOR YOUR
NEXT CONFERENCE ?

Doug West and Cheryl Cappellano bring you a unique, dynamic and inspirational 60 minute presentation bringing the audience the same down-to-earth and practical personal growth strategies contained in the new book "It's Your Frog ... Warts and All."

Participants will enjoy hearing Doug and Cheryl talk about:

▸ Thoughts That Go Bump In The Night
▸ Change Is The 500 Pound Gorilla
▸ Getting A Little More Out Of The Most You Have
▸ The Waiters And The Doers
▸ Sharing A Vision
▸ Nobody Plays With My Lego Anymore

Call
1 800 265-4249